IN THE

"The Impala, tryin[g] [to get] past me. Jo[hn Goins was firing] from the front of the car, and Griffen was firing from the backseat. Because of the angle of the Chrysler, they had maybe half a second to get me as they drove past. I returned fire and hit Goins in the head. The Impala skidded wildly . . ."

"I remember thinking, 'Oh my God, I've been shot in the head . . .' I stood there, surrounded by all those people, frantically slapping the right side of my head, trying to find the bullet hole. I must have looked like a crazy man . . ."

"You must never let a hostage situation go any longer than is necessary. In other words, if you have the opportunity to stop it, you better stop it. It isn't a time for talking. It's a time for action . . ."

BADGE OF VALOR

JOSEPH A. WEST

BERKLEY BOOKS, NEW YORK

Grateful acknowledgment is made to R. D. Brooks for permission to print excerpts from his song, "The Ballad of Stan Guffey."

BADGE OF VALOR

A Berkley Book/published by arrangement with
the author

PRINTING HISTORY
Berkley edition/December 1993

ISBN: 0-425-14014-8

BERKLEY®
Berkley Books are published by The Berkley Publishing Group,
200 Madison Avenue, New York, New York 10016.
BERKLEY and the "B" design
are trademarks belonging to Berkley Publishing Corporation.

PRINTED IN THE UNITED STATES OF AMERICA

10 9 8 7 6 5 4 3 2 1

For
Emily
and
Alex

ACKNOWLEDGMENTS

The following people and organizations were of great assistance to me in gathering the material for this book, and I owe them all a debt of gratitude:

Sandra King of the Pompano, Florida, Police Department; Massad Ayoob, Director of the Lethal Force Institute of Concord, New Hampshire; Texas Ranger Historian Mike Cox; Craig W. Floyd of the National Law Enforcement Officers Memorial; Calibre Press of Northbrook, Illinois, who allowed me to make use of their wonderful video, *Ultimate Survivors*: *Winning Against Incredible Odds*; The Federal Bureau of Investigation; The Department of the Interior; and The Bureau of Indian Affairs.

I would also like to thank the hundreds of men and women in law enforcement I've spoken with over the past year. All of them helped make *Badge of Valor* possible.

Last, and by no means least, I wish to thank my wife, without whose patience, talent and understanding this book could not have been written.

INTRODUCTION

■■■■■■■■■■■■■■■■■■■■■

About a year ago this fall, I was practicing with my old .44.40 Colt Single Action Army at a police and civilian shooting range near Palm Beach Gardens, Florida.

After the buzzer sounded that declared the range "cold," a grizzled old retired deputy sheriff, who had been tearing dead-center chest out of a man-sized silhouette target with his finely tuned .45 Smith and Wesson service pistol, eyeballed my piece and said:

"What kinda ol' hawgleg is that, mister?"

I told him. Then added lamely, "I'm not much of a shooter, but I like the old Colt because I'm interested in the Old West. I think maybe I'll write a book someday."

The deputy feigned surprise, spat and said, "Y'all mean a book about gunfighters and gunfightin' an' sich?"

I allowed that this was indeed the case.

The old lawman spat again, fished in his pocket for change, then dropped fifty cents into the soda pop machine. He punched a button and scooped up the Diet Sprite that clattered into the hatch.

"When was that hawgleg made?" he asked mildly. He popped the tab of his drink, and Sprite splashed over his hand, a hairy, red-hued mitt that looked as big as a Virginia smoked ham.

I watched him drink, and having failed to find his eyes behind his dark shooting glasses, I spoke to his bobbing Adam's apple. "My records show that the Colt factory shipped the gun to a hardware store in Austin, Texas, in April, 1886," I said.

"Listen, mister," the old man said. "Old West, my ass. There's more gunfightin' an' killin' an' dyin' and good men droppin' in the street now—today—than there ever was when that ol' fuckin' relic cost twelve bucks in a Texas hardware store.

"Every day. Every single passing day, cops are killing and being killed in gunfights that would make your fuckin' hair stand on end. You know what gunfightin' is?"

I shook my head. "Well, not really. I—"

"I'll tell you what gunfightin' is. What gunfightin' is to a modern-day cop. Gunfightin' is pulling your piece, an' you're as scared as hell, an' stickin' it right into a guy's belly and pullin' the trigger. There's blood and guts everywhere, and it's all over your gun and it's all over your hands, but you keep on shooting till the bastard goes down, because that way he'll die an' you'll live an' you'll see your wife and kids again.

"An' after it's all over, an' the poor fucker's been taken away to the morgue or wherever, your fellow officers will slap you on the back and say you done good. An' you'll just stand there, shakin' all over, an' you'll say that you don't feel so fuckin' good. You've just killed a man, seen the light go out of his eyes, an' that will stay with you for the rest of your life. Sometimes it'll hurt so bad, you'll feel sick in the stomach for months. Sometimes you'll go to drinkin' an' never stop. Maybe your marriage will break up, an' maybe you'll go out with other women, an' you'll be a dud in the sack because your fuckin' sex drive is all shot to hell."

The old man took a deep breath, drained his soda can, crushed it into a shapeless ball and tossed it in the garbage can. "That's what fuckin' gunfightin' is. Today. This minute. Put that in your fuckin' book, mister."

The old deputy fished in his shirt pocket and found a crumpled pack of Marlboros. He pulled out a bent cigarette, straightened it with huge fingers and lighted the smoke with a battered Zippo that had a Marine Corps emblem on the side. He looked past me to the range office, tilted back his head and yelled: "Hey, Tom! You gonna make this fuckin' range hot ever again? Or are we all just gonna pack our guns away an' join hands an' play ring around the fuckin' rosie."

Tom told the old man to hold his horses and that there were *other* dues-paying people on the range besides him and they wanted to check their targets and why was he in such an all fired *hurry* anyhow, it wasn't like he'd important places to go.

"Yeah, yeah," the old deputy said. "Back at ya." Then under his breath: "Place is full of fuckin' pansies."

This unhappy thought brought him back, reluctantly it seemed, to me. "You ever visited the National Law Enforcement Officers Memorial in Virginia?" he asked.

I replied in the negative.

"I been there. I was there when it was dedicated. They got two 304-foot-long marble walls, an' they got the names of the 12,561 law enforcement officers who have died in the line of duty since 1794.

"Know what's sad about them walls? I'll tell you. They made them walls so they'd hold 29,233 names, so half of the space is blank. Every year, 153 cops, deputies and others are killed in the line of duty, so they'll be adding names to them walls till the year 2100. That's what's fuckin' sad about them walls.

"The money for the memorial came from the general public, hundreds of thousands of them. The government didn't give a single fuckin' red cent. You want to write a book? Write about the cops on them walls, or write about the cop heroes who are riskin' their lives every fuckin' day. That's what people are interested in. Not Wyatt fuckin' Earp."

The range buzzer suddenly cut across the old man's soliloquy, telling us that the range was hot. He raised his nickled Smith and Wesson and sent a flurry of shots downrange. Then he expertly dropped the magazine, looked at me sadly and shook his head. "Old West my ass."

He didn't speak again.

That conversation prompted me to do some initial research, and I discovered that there is indeed a thin, blue line out there where blazing gunfights, sudden, violent death and almost unbelievable bravery are commonplace.

Extreme bravery is becoming so routine, so expected of a law enforcement officer, that it prompted this exchange between myself and a desk sergeant when I called a large police department in Arizona.

"We haven't had much happen recently," the sergeant said. "We had one officer that got shot seven times during a holdup attempt. He's lying there bleeding, but he sat up and shot one of the bad guys dead center and wounded the other. Then we had an officer pull some kids out of a burning building. He got burned up pretty bad, because he went in there three times.

"But we haven't had anything you would say was real heroic."

Today, Texas Rangers are still dying; big city cops, many of them women, are killing and being killed among the shadows of a nightmare underworld, made terrible by drugs, poverty and hopelessness; and the deputy sheriff, that living symbol of the Old West, is still being cut down in a hail of gunfire, often in places where the air is clean and a tall man can look across the desert for miles.

There are currently 1.7 million men and women directly or indirectly involved in law enforcement in this country, and the stories of guts, determination and raw courage among them are legion.

They are paid, modestly to be sure, to walk *toward* danger, while the rest of us flee from it. At a time when Americans are becoming less and less inclined to take any kind of risk, our law enforcement officers walk *toward* guns and knives in the hands of crazed dope addicts, *toward* burning buildings, *toward* ticking bombs and blazing cars. *Toward* fear. *Toward* terror. *Toward* the unknown.

And in exchange for all this . . . we call them *pigs*.

I interviewed hundreds of law enforcement officers in the course of writing this book. Not one of them could be described as a trigger-happy lout. In fact, most officers will use their weapons reluctantly, and then only as a last resort. A cop knows that firing his service weapon immediately puts him in a no-win situation. If he makes the wrong decision, shoots the wrong person at the wrong time, it can destroy his career. Even if he shoots the right person at the right time for the right reason, he can still suffer. He will be suspended from duty, or set to paper shuffling in headquarters, while an investigation is carried out—often aided and abetted by an eager media—that will be conducted from the very outset as though he were a criminal. And if the bad guy survives, he will sue the cop for civil rights violations. If the officer gets through all this, and gets into another shooting scrape, he will be forever branded as a troublemaker and routinely passed over for promotion.

Bear all this in mind when you meet the men and women in this book. They are not merely faceless uniforms. They are people just like you and me. They care, often deeply, about the public they are sworn to protect, and uphold the lofty principles of law enforcement with courage, commitment and compassion. All of them have proven that they are quite willing to lay down their lives for these principles.

Most of these men and women hold the Medal of Valor,

or have been named Police Officer of the Year, our nation's top award in law enforcement.

Within the pages of this book they tell their stories in their own words. They tell them matter of factly, without false heroics and without embellishment.

These cops, from FBI special agents, to Texas rangers, to Nevada sheriffs to Blackfeet Indian officers, are the bravest people I have ever met. I feel honored to have known them and to have shared a small part of their lives, however briefly.

Our law enforcement officers have often been reviled by an ungrateful society, killed and maimed by ruthless criminals and all but forgotten by a public that didn't seem to care.

I hope and pray that this book will help change all of that.

There is one thing more. There is a slim possibility that the retired deputy I spoke of earlier will read this volume. For that reason let me hastily add that, although I was a cop for many years, I know little of guns and gunfighting. I have never been in a gunfight, and I know I would mess up horribly if I ever were. When I write of guns, gunfights and gunfighters, I am only passing on what others, infinitely more knowledgeable, have told me.

In short, I am merely a troubadour plucking the harp string and reciting the valiant deeds of men and women much braver than myself.

JEFF HALL
Alaska State Troopers

■ ■

"**W**e've been hit! We've been hit! Break off! Break off!" Captain Don Lawrence's voice, hard-edged, metallic with sudden, overwhelming tension and the stress of being on the losing end of a one-sided firefight, jarred through the intercom, the words cutting into State Trooper Jeff Hall's consciousness like rusty scalpels. As Hall fought to bring his rifle on target through the open window of the helicopter, he was desperately aware that beside him pilot Tom Davis was wrestling with the controls of the big chopper, the flaring blades skidding through the thin, cold Alaska air as the aircraft clawed for altitude. The cabin was a charnel house. The Plexiglas was splashed bright crimson from the blood and brains of the dead trooper slumped in the seat beside Lawrence. The dead man was tall, lanky Troy Duncan, a Texas-born former Marine captain—and the most accurate rifle shot in the elite Alaska State Trooper Special Emergency Response Team, the equivalent of the police SWAT unit.

Jeff Hall knew that as a marksman he was very much playing second best as he sighted his M-16 at the man on the riverbank. He had already missed badly with an eight-round burst of tracer, hitting low and to the left, kicking up dirt around the man's feet. In the split second before he died, Troy Duncan, superb rifle shot though he was, had also missed clean.

Hall now sighted a second time, fully aware that the lives of the two men with him in the chopper were on the line. The crazed killer on the ground, a drifter and would-be mountain man named Michael Silka, had already proved himself to be a cold and ruthless gunfighter and a lethal expert with his .30.06 Ruger rifle.

The chattering chopper was still vainly battling for altitude as Captain Lawrence's white-knuckled hands gripped the back of the pilot's seat and he yelled again: "Get us out of here!"

Lawrence had been shaken badly when he'd seen Duncan's head explode under the terrifying impact of Silka's bullet. He had been splashed by blood and brains, and hit and slightly wounded in the face, as the .30.06 round fragmented. But, a product of his training and mental conditioning, the captain showed no fear in his voice, just the unbelieving, anguished roar of a senior officer who had been struck by the awful realization that he had one man down and that his little command was now in desperate peril.

Hall meantime watched Silka bring up his deadly rifle for another shot. The trooper swallowed hard. "Oh Jesus," he thought. "This is it. You can't miss this time, Jeff. You can't miss." The young cop, white-faced, his lips snarled back from his teeth by overwhelming stress and fear, fought down his rising panic. He took a deep, steadying breath, laid the sights of the M-16 on Silka's chest—and fired . . .

■   ■   ■

The countdown to that desperate, bloody air battle had begun a few weeks before, in mid-May 1984, when long-haired, bearded Michael Silka drove his beat-up brown

Dodge sedan, a canoe tied to the roof, into Manley Hot Springs, Alaska.

The five-foot-eleven, 160-pound twenty-five-year-old arrived in the picturesque Tanana Valley town of rustic log cabins and quaint turn-of-the-century stores by way of a tortuous, rutted 165-mile road that cut directly into the heart of the state from Fairbanks to the west. The community in the mid-eighties was home to some seventy people, mostly taciturn trappers, fishermen and husky-mushers.

To the locals, people like Silka were end-of-the-roaders, born-again losers who had gone to see the guru on the mountaintop and the aging flower children in San Francisco, but failed to find whatever their restless souls were seeking or to exorcise the personal demons that tormented them. They finally ended up in Alaska, many of them, our nation's last frontier. They took the road from Fairbanks till it petered out in Manley Hot Springs, and there they stopped. There was nowhere else to go. This was the end of the line. Beyond Manley there was nothing but hundreds of miles of wilderness and death in a thousand forms.

Silka, a brooding, jobless loner and soon-to-be ruthless mass murderer, was an Army veteran who dreamed of being a mountain man. His fascination with guns had earned him a police record at an early age, and when he drove into Manley Springs he might already have made his first kill. He is suspected of shooting a man named Roger Culp in Fairbanks.

"He was scraggly and he acted real weird," says longtime Manley resident Patricia Lee, who then operated the local roadhouse. "He seemed to be a typical end-of-the-roader, just another of the weirdos who end up here."

Another resident, Teresa Conger, recalls that during her only meeting with Silka he kept fussing with a huge Bowie knife. "He had that huge knife, and he kept sharpening and sharpening it. It seemed to me he was just obsessed with that knife."

A day after the killing of Roger Culp, two Alaska state troopers had paid a visit to Silka's shack at a rural settlement on the outskirts of Fairbanks named Hopkinsville, just two miles from the residence of Senator Frank Murkowski, where President and Mrs. Reagan sometimes vacationed.

Trooper Mike Pullen and Wildlife Protection Officer Paul Richards were checking out a report of blood puddles and a suspicious snow-covered mound near Silka's cabin.

Pullen remembers being especially tense as he and Richards pulled up at Silka's wood and tar-paper shack around 6:35 P.M. on April 29, 1984.

"Richards must have felt the same way," he recalls, "because he tossed me an extra set of car keys and said, 'If anything happens to me, you can get out of here and get help.'"

The troopers had been sent to the area to check out the two main possibilities for the blood—a homicide or a moose poaching.

They knocked on Silka's door, and there was no answer. The two men walked around the cabin and saw the mound of snow, which was round, not oblong, and only about three feet in diameter. The lawmen then poked around in the mound and came up with a bloody, folded-over moose hide.

Pullen dug down to ground level, but found nothing else. "I can't say for sure, but I knew in my intuition that the body of Culp wasn't there," he says.

The two officers went back to the front of the shack and banged on the door. This time Silka answered. "Who's there?"

Pullen identified himself as a state trooper. "I want to talk to you."

"Are you alone?" Silka asked.

No," Pullen replied, "I have another officer with me."

Silka stuck his head and half his body through the door. Pullen could not see the man's right hand.

"The more I think about it, the more I know what was in that hand," Pullen says. "If only one of us had been out there, that trooper would be dead."

The trooper says he spoke to Silka "for no more than five minutes."

"He said he'd been keeping some moose hide during the winter for hunter friends, and had washed the blood off with water," Pullen says. "When we found some hides out drying, it all seemed plausible at the time."

Richards recalls that Silka "looked like he was on drugs," and he "wasn't surprised" by Silka's hostile attitude.

"You got to remember that the Hopkinsville natives are not members of the Kiwanis Club," he says. "That's not one of the places where you'd go and be welcomed with open arms by the local populace."

The two officers left Silka and went back to their station without talking to any of the neighbors.

There the case rested until May 7, when a woman came forward and said that she'd seen Silka "go off with Roger Culp" and had then heard two gunshots.

On May 8, troopers went to the Silka shack armed with a search warrant and found the place deserted. The officers took samples of the blood around the cabin and sent it off to the state lab in Palmer for analysis. On May 14, the day after Silka arrived in Manley, the lab said the samples looked like human blood. On May 16—the day before Silka spread death and terror in the little community, killing seven innocent people including a pregnant woman and her two-year-old son—the lab confirmed that the blood was definitely human.

The troopers were now convinced that Silka had killed Culp and somehow disposed of his body, possibly in the frozen Tanana River. An all-points bulletin for the arrest of the suspected killer went out to trooper posts around the state and to Canadian border stations.

But it was too late. Silka, who was now a proven and deadly gunman, had already taken the loser's road to Manley Hot Springs, his Dodge loaded up with the high-powered rifles and heavy-caliber revolvers he worshiped.

Silka showed up in town on Mother's Day, May 13.

Though he struck most people as being a little odd, he didn't seem violent or any weirder than a host of other end-of-the-roaders who had briefly called the settlement home.

"We get the dregs of society coming through here all the time," one longtime resident recalls. "They come. They stay awhile, then they leave. Most times, nobody pays them any mind when they're here, nobody notices when they leave and nobody regrets their going."

Silka, who set up camp near the town boat landing and close-by garbage dump, told some people he had come to fish for bass and muskie, species unknown in the waters around Manley. He told others he could smell clams through six feet of water. "Smell 'em all the way down there, then dig 'em up and sell 'em," he said. "There's good money in clams."

The younger male residents of the town thought the newcomer was full of shit.

Resident Dorothy Zoller recalls that on Tuesday, May 14, Silka talked to her about staking a homestead.

"He discussed being in the service and thought he could make some Army points that would make it easier for him to stake some land," she says.

Silka had a seventeen-foot aluminum canoe on top of his car, and they talked about that. They also talked about Silka's well-honed Bowie knife.

"Ain't she a beauty," Silka said. "You can skin out a grizzly with a knife like that or chop wood or do anything with it. This here is a gen-u-ine Bowie. They don't make knives like this anymore."

"Silka was real nice looking, except for his long beard and hair," Zoller says. "He had his shirt off, and he looked fit and muscular."

The woman says she didn't feel threatened by Silka. Just the opposite. "I felt some sympathy for him, because I'd just gone through the hassle of getting land myself."

But when Zoller met Silka at the landing the next day, he didn't say a word. He walked up to her truck, seemed to think better of it and walked away. Zoller thought that "maybe I had wakened him."

But when she met him again on Wednesday, Silka was talkative and even asked about the people in the settlement and the local gossip.

"I guess nothing much happens in a place like this, nothing exciting that is," he said. He smiled.

Then on Thursday, May 27, a day of horror the people of Manley will not soon forget, Silka was quiet again. He spent the early morning working on an old Evinrude engine, which he hoped to attach to his canoe.

"He walked up to me, and I thought he was going to say something, then he just turned around and walked away," Zoller says.

Gwen Evans says Silka "acted as if he saw right through me when I said hello. It was like I was a puff of wind that went by."

Later, between two and three that afternoon, seven other people went to the boat landing. All of them died.

Joe McVey, thirty-seven, a Vietnam veteran who came home wounded and sometimes wore metal braces on his legs, and twenty-four-year-old Dale Madajski went there to try to float McVey's boat. One of these two men had what the Alaska State Troopers later described as "an abrasive personality." It was to get him killed that day.

The troopers believe that Silka and the two men got into an argument, probably over Silka's assertion that he was going to do a Daniel Boone and become a mountain man.

Like many a drifter before him, Silka planned to head into the Alaskan heartland and trap beaver. A man could also pan for gold up in the mountain streams, and if he was careful maybe hit enough paydirt to buy supplies and rifle bullets and powder. But either McVey or Madajski, we will never know which, said something like: "Aw, you're full of shit!"

It was precisely the wrong thing to say to a skilled, psychopathic gunman with an easily bruised ego.

Stung, Silka grabbed a Ruger .44-magnum carbine from his car and shot McVey above the right eye. The man was dead when he hit the ground. Madajski, unarmed and terribly afraid, ran for his life. He had only gone a few steps when Silka dropped him with a bullet to the head.

Madajski and his pretty young wife, Kirstin, were from Minnesota and had been preparing to move to Fairbanks in a few weeks with their twelve-month-old baby.

Minutes later twenty-seven-year-old Albert Hagen went down to the dump near the boat landing with a load of brush. Hagen's parents were Manley old-timers and had operated a sawmill there for two decades, but the young man had spent the last ten years away from the community, fishing commercially off the California coast. He had returned to Manley only a month before.

Silka killed him.

The gunman, long-haired and wild-eyed, was dragging Hagen's body into the Tanana River when thirty-one-year-old Lyman Klein, his thirty-year-old wife, Joyce, then two months pregnant, and their two-year-old son, Marshall, drove their four-wheeled ATV down to the landing. No one will ever know why they happened to be there. The residents of Manley speculate that Lyman Klein and his young family were just taking a ride to enjoy the scenery along the riverbank.

The Kleins were newcomers to Manley, quiet and deeply religious. They had built two cabins "and hoped to sell one to the people who were renting it," so they could build another house farther upriver.

Whatever their reason for being there, they blundered into a scene of unspeakable horror. Silka was just dragging the body of his last victim into the river when the Kleins arrived.

"What are you doing?" Lyman Klein demanded. "Who have you got there?"

His wife, suddenly very afraid, whispered: "Lyman, let's get out of here now. I don't like this."

Blam! Blam! Blam! It took only three racketing shots from Silka's deadly Ruger carbine, and three more bodies were dragged into the ice-cold water.

Silka then calmly loaded up his canoe and paddled east on the Tanana. He didn't look back. He was smiling. He was off to be a mountain man.

Bob Lee, owner of the Manley Roadhouse, says Alice McVey, Joe's wife, "became very concerned" when she went to the landing later that evening and found her husband's boat still there. There was a six-pack of beer in his truck, not the kind of thing he'd leave behind.

Kristin Madajski "wondered" about her husband too, and Albert and Bea Hagen were worried about their son.

But the weather had been wonderfully warm, creeping into the low forties, and relatives assumed the missing people "had just gone off somewhere." McVey had a camp across the river where he kept a dozen sled dogs, and McVey's wife thought that her husband might have gone there.

But on Friday, May 18, at 2 P.M. Alice McVey, now thoroughly alarmed, called the troopers in Fairbanks. The troopers realized that concern was mounting fast in Manley, but all they knew was that some people from the town were overdue from their various outings.

Friends and family of the missing gathered at the Hagen house to await news, drawing near to one another, finding comfort in the presence of others who were also worried about their loved ones.

By evening, someone thought to check the license plate of the stranger's car, which was still at the landing.

"Maybe that poor guy is missing too," a voice in the Hagen house said.

Sometime between ten and midnight Friday, residents can't remember exactly when, the license number was phoned in to the troopers. It matched the plate of Michael Silka, who was being sought for the murder of Roger Culp of Fairbanks. The troopers told everyone in Manley to be on guard, and that they would be out as soon as possible. They arrived at the settlement at 2 A.M. Saturday morning, and in the gray twilight the helicopters were already cutting through the air above the little town.

Trooper Jeff Hall of the Special Emergency Response Team had been rousted out of bed at midnight when his pager went off, its jangling, insistent beeping driving him quickly to the telephone. He was told that this was not a practice response test, but the real thing.

"Get down to the office quick," he was ordered.

On the bed, Hall's girlfriend, soon to be his wife, woke with a drowsy slowness. "Wha . . . what's happening?" she asked sleepily.

"Nothing much," the young trooper said. "Some kind of flap going on about an escaped murderer. Routine stuff." He kissed the woman on the forehead. "Go back to sleep, honey. I'll call you later."

"I grabbed my gear, jumped in my car and drove down to the office," Hall recalls. "There were some other SERT guys there, and Sam Bernard, the homicide sergeant, gave us the briefing.

"Sam had been a SERT team leader for years, and he was the best homicide investigator the department ever had. Sam told us that there were a bunch of people missing in Manley Hot Springs and that Michael Silka had been in the area.

"We're gonna go get that guy," Sam said.

Hall and four other troopers, including tall, handsome Troy Duncan, were flown into Manley by fixed-wing aircraft, arriving there at around three in the morning.

"In May, at that time in the morning, it's almost light," Hall says. "We all piled into a pickup truck and drove down to about a mile from the landing. Then we got out and approached the place on foot.

"When we got to the landing, the place was deserted. There were some abandoned buildings close by, and we made a sweep of those and found nothing.

"The river was open, all the ice melted, and Silka's canoe was gone. There were bloodstains on the ground and some empty .44-magnum shell casings lying around. We called Fairbanks and told them to get the homicide guys down here right away. 'And get us a helicopter,' Captain Lawrence said."

Hall, Duncan and Lawrence were airborne by 4 A.M. and flew a search pattern along the Tanana till 10, when they stopped to refuel.

"After we refueled, we headed to the hunting camps strung out along the riverbanks," Hall says. "It was bear season and a lot of hunters were out. We warned them that Silka was in the area, gave them a description and told them to be on the lookout."

Later, heavily armed troopers were dropped off at many of the more isolated hunting camps as an extra precaution.

At one of these remote camps, a grinning hunter slapped the stock of his .270 Winchester and told a trooper: "Hell, if that guy comes into my camp, ol' Betsy here will take care of him. I ain't afraid of no hippy end-of-the-roader."

The trooper just smiled. "If he comes, be very afraid of him," he said. "This guy is enough to scare any man."

"Aw hell," the hunter said, "he doesn't scare me none." But the man wasn't grinning any longer, and he took to looking over his shoulder for the rest of the day.

Meanwhile Silka, now in fevered pursuit of his twisted dream, met trapper Fred Burke, twenty-seven, on the river. Burke, known to his friends as "Weeds," maintained three camps on the Tanana, moving from one to the other depending on the season. On this, the last day of his life, the quiet, soft-spoken outdoorsman was heading for Manley to repair the clutch on a pickup truck he'd left there.

According to the Reverend Les Zerbe, who was later to conduct the young man's funeral service, Burke had prayed at dinner on the day before he died "that he had in mind for his whole family that if God wanted to do whatever it takes for us to become more aware of Him in our life, then let it happen."

Burke, a deeply religious, God-fearing man, was to have no time for a final prayer.

He may have hailed Silka, asking him where he was headed. The river was clear of ice, and the weather was warm.

Silka didn't reply. All he wanted was Burke's boat and gasoline. He brought the Ruger carbine to his shoulder, fired and saw Burke's body jerk under the impact of the .44-magnum bullet. The young trapper's body splashed into the water and vanished from sight. Silka then tied his canoe to the stern of Burke's powerboat and left the Tanana, turning due south along its tributary the Zitziana River, heading into the wild Alaskan heartland—and freedom.

But at four that afternoon, Alaska state troopers flying a Piper Cub spotted the fugitive at a slough about a hundred river miles upstream from Manley and flashed a message to Captain Lawrence, telling him to hustle his two-helicopter task force to the area. Fast!

"We're on our way," Lawrence said. Then to Hall and Duncan: "I think we've got him, boys."

"Our plan was to drop off a couple of troopers who would approach the slough on foot," Hall says. "Our choppers would then circle behind Silka, hover above him and to the rear, so we'd have him boxed in within a triangle of firepower.

"Unfortunately, in this business things never seem to work out the way they're planned."

In the command helicopter, Lawrence quickly saw that Silka was holed up within fifty yards of the only landing zone in the area.

"That's heavily timbered country out there, mostly birch and spruce, and there were a lot of ridges around the riverbanks," Hall says. "Silka had the one suitable LZ covered, so we went to plan B, which was to drop a trooper to the ground and have him secure the LZ till we could land the chopper."

But because of the terrain and the close proximity of Silka, a known and deadly marksman, that plan was also scrubbed.

Silka was concealed behind an earth berm and covered by three birch trees that were growing out of the cutbank at an angle. Burke's boat was tied to one of these trees, and Silka's canoe was tied to the boat. The gunman held a Ruger Number One B Standard sporting rifle in his hands, with a 4-power scope. The eight-pound rifle is a classic falling-block single shot in .30.06 caliber. Silka held five extra rounds of his own 180-grain reloads in his mouth, and so great was his skill and speed he could get off one aimed shot a second. He had once demonstrated this skill to some of the Manley old-timers, keeping a tin can bouncing along in front of him as he walked behind it, firing his single-shot Ruger like a semi-automatic. This was truly superb gun handling by any standard.

"As we flew along the river, we saw Silka get his rifle from the boat," Hall says. "Then we lost sight of him. We circled around, and Tom Davidson, a former gunship pilot and crop duster, brought us into the wind. We were going to drop into the only LZ in the area, the one covered by Silka's rifle!

"Tom flared the chopper and we started to drop. But I keyed the mike and yelled: 'No, no, go hot! Go hot! He's got the LZ covered!' I was afraid that when we made our final flare we'd be stationary in the aircraft for a few seconds. Sitting targets."

The pilot gunned the chopper, battling for altitude, but now the troopers were a fat, inviting target, flying at treetop level just fifty yards from Silka's position.

Silka, outnumbered and outgunned, nevertheless did a remarkable thing—he attacked!

"Here was a guy with a single-shot rifle attacking two helicopters full of SWAT guys," Hall marvels. "You're talking about a guy who was both physically and mentally prepared for combat. A guy so focused, so intent on his dream, that he was not going to let anything stand in his way.

"As we tried to gain height, Silka swung up his rifle and fired. Troy Duncan also fired. And I let loose with an eight-round burst from my M-16. We all missed.

"Troy was a former Marine Corps marksman, and he had his scoped M-16 in semi-automatic mode. He was careful. He wanted a good cheek-to-stock weld. A good sight picture. Nice, even pressure on the trigger and a good, crisp, one-shot kill. But he never had time to make that textbook-perfect shot. Silka's next round killed him.

"Troy's head seemed to explode when the bullet hit. I

heard Captain Lawrence, who was bleeding from a wound in his face, yelling to the pilot to get us out of there.

"The helicopter was skidding through the air, still trying to gain height. I expected a bullet to shatter my head at any second. I knew Silka was that good. He was very, very good. There was a lot of noise on the intercom now, from both helicopters, people yelling, shouting questions, bellowing advice. My mouth was bone dry. I brought my rifle up, laid the sights on Silka, breathed a silent prayer—and squeezed the trigger . . ."

Hall had missed before. But now all of his training and remarkable, steadfast courage paid off. He fired the remainder of his magazine at Silka, some twenty rounds, and saw the tracers vanish wickedly into the long-haired gunman's body.

"I had hit low and to the left before," Hall says, "but this time I hit him with eight rounds. My bullets struck Silka in the lower leg, then the body and right arm, and two crashed through his head.

"I saw him throw his rifle high into the air, and he went backwards into the slough. His head was underwater and his feet were on the bank. I punched out the magazine and slammed another 30-rounder into the M-16, preparing to shoot again. But Silka was down, and he wasn't getting up ever again. The entire gun battle, from the first shot to the last, had taken just 2.2 seconds.

"I heard Captain Lawrence yell: 'We're hit! We're hit! Break off! Break off!'

"Then our communications totally went all to shit.

"The other helicopter was right behind us. They'd stopped off earlier to leave a trooper with some bear hunters and had played catch up. They were just seconds behind us, close enough to see the water boiling around Silka as my rounds hit him.

"Now it seemed that everybody was talking at once,

wanting to know about the firefight, asking who had done the shooting and who was hurt. For the first time since the fight began, I looked behind me and saw that Troy Duncan, that gallant Marine and first-rate trooper and my friend for many years, would never again be at my side.

"Beside me, the pilot was taking us home. I felt drained. Physically and emotionally exhausted. But I wanted to go back to the slough, back to where Michael Silka was. I wanted to cut his head off."

　　　　　　■　　　■　　　■

Troy Duncan, married, the father of two children, was later posthumously awarded the Alaska State Troopers Medal of Valor.

Jeff Hall, now a sergeant and still a member of the Special Emergency Response Team, was commended for bravery above and beyond the call of duty.

Silka's four-hour rampage in Manley Hot Springs is still fresh in the memory of the people who live there. The carnage chilled the soul of the community, perhaps warping it, changing it forever.

After Silka was killed, the townspeople realized he was now beyond their reach, so they took out their terrible frustration on his car, which he had abandoned near the bloody dock.

They got their guns, axes and sledgehammers and shot up and hammered at the brown Dodge, tearing it to pieces before throwing it in the river.

It didn't help much.

Now only time, a lot of time, will heal Manley's wounds.

OFFICERS ALAN JOHNSON AND VERNICE BROWN
Pompano Beach, Florida, Police Department

■■■■■■■■■■■■■■■■■■■■■

Gunfighting is at best a chancy business, and the prudent man, cop or civilian, avoids it like the plague. There are no hard and fast rules and too many variables to reliably predict the outcome of an armed encounter with large-caliber handguns. Modern gunfights, using semiautomatic weapons, last on an average between three and five seconds, usually at ranges of five feet and under, and as many as thirty rounds can be fired in less time than it takes the second hand of a watch to go from twelve to one. But once committed to the gunfight, in other words if there is no other way out of it—including running away—the very skilled and very lucky gunfighter will sometimes walk from the scene unscathed. The less skilled or less lucky loser ends up dead almighty quick.

Our police and the legally armed citizen depend on firing-range training and the crucial mental conditioning that make for success and victory in a sudden, violent, armed confrontation. They accept the reality that we live in a dangerous world and that there *really are* criminals out there who will try to rape, rob, torture, terrorize and kill you. Cop and civilian alike, if they're ready and game, know they might one day meet one of these creatures and have to fight for their lives.

But the vicious criminal predator, and oh my God there are an awful lot of them, has one serious advantage over the rest of us: He is always ready and willing to kill, cripple and destroy without mercy and without remorse.

Normal people, the police included, lack this mind-set, so that no matter how polished their gunfighting skills, they many times find themselves at a terrible disadvantage in violent confrontation with the predatory armed criminal.

Then too there is the unending confusion and conflicting advice that exists among the experts about what weapon to bring to a gunfight and how to use the damned piece once you get there.

"Boy, you keep your eye on that there front sight, no matter what the range, or you're gonna get yer ass shot up an' get yesse'f kilt," says one. And the obedient rookie nods his head.

Says another: "Boy, you forget that there front sight in a close-range gunfight and point the piece like you was pointing a finger, or you're gonna get your ass shot up and get yesse'f kilt."

And a third will advise: "Boy, you jest hold that piece down at waist level in both hands, elbows close in to your sides, an' then cut loose, or you're gonna get yer ass shot up an' get yesse'f kilt."

Then there's the "expert" who will tell the wide-eyed rookie: "Boy, you carry anything else to a gunfight except a high-capacity 9mm an' you're gonna get yer ass shot up an' get yesse'f kilt."

"Naw," says another, "fergit that there fancy 9mm crunchenticker. Boy, if'n you ain't using a good ol', big ol' Colt's .45, you can bet the bank you're gonna get yer ass shot up an' get yess'f kilt."

And there's always this one: "Fergit them autoloaders, son. You get yesse'f a handy-dandy .357 Smith an' Wesson, see, an' load it up with them there surplus Israeli army

125-grain, extra-pointy, titanium-jacketed, diamond-tipped, fragmentin', explodin' hollowpoints or you're gonna get your ass shot up an' get yesse'f kilt."

Enough already!

The wise man knows that his chances of winning any gunfight (this means putting the bad guy out of action and walking away with your own hide at least reasonably intact) are as good as tossing a coin in the air and having it come down heads—it's a fifty-fifty proposition. And in gunfighting, those are miserable odds.

Imagine then the courage, the complete mastery of the natural fear response, of two police officers who could have ducked the lethal uncertainty of the gunfight, let it lay, stepped away from it without anyone pointing a finger of blame in their direction, yet who—out of a sense of responsibility to others and their own deep sense of duty—weighed the alternatives and deliberately chose to put themselves in harm's way.

Officers Alan Johnson and Vernice Brown of the Pompano Beach Police in Florida, are both thirty-three years old, tall, muscular, athletic black men, handsome as movie stars, with the star's physical presence, so that when they are together they seem to fill up the room. They share a ready intelligence and immediate grasp of detail which has been honed to near razor sharpness by their department's state-of-the-art training programs.

Both men are members of the Raiders, Pompano's crack street narcotics team. Until the blazing gunfight that catapulted the two officers into the media limelight and won them the nation's top police award for bravery, they had patrolled one of the world's toughest neighborhoods in relative obscurity. Residents knew who they were, but the rest of the city did not. In the dark, echoing hours of the graveyard shift, Johnson and Brown and the others in their seventeen-man unit busted crack dealers, stormed drug hangouts, sweet-talked informants and cracked codes for "beeper dope," which, true to its name, can be bought by digital beeper. Such is progress. Then, as now, the job was dirty, risky, downright discouraging—and without so much as a shred of even tattered glory.

Brown is the more outgoing of the two, with a quick, easy smile and a relaxed, friendly manner that instantly puts the stranger at ease. He does most of the talking for the partnership, and loves to tell you about his wife and children and their hopes for the future, the cost of college, how he worries about the influences that shape a kid's growing up. He drops his kids off at school in the morning and will cut a U-turn to a pay phone when his wife Sherril calls him via his beeper to ask directions to tonight's high school football game or just to say, as she does every day: "I love you."

Officer Johnson is also a family man, but he's quieter, more intense, with a prizefighter's wide-shouldered, narrow-hipped physique and the easy, catlike grace and quick, graceful movement of the born athlete and gunfighter. He carries a stainless steel, Smith and Wesson Model 645 .45-caliber autoloader, stuffed with 158-grain Federal Hydra-Shoks, high on his right side, higher than most, and like Brown, he professes to have little or no affection for the piece.

"A gun like this is just a tool," he says. "A tool to get the job done. I don't think about it much. It's just there. I practice with it. I clean it. But I don't think about it much."

Johnson and Brown patrol a crime-ridden, inner-city neighborhood in Pompano, cruising the depressed northwest section of town in an unmarked police car. Their uniform, or lack of it, consists of blue jeans, sneakers and a black T-shirt with "POLICE" on the front. They wear a mesh vest over the shirt, and this also says, "POLICE." Their gunbelts are standard issue, black leather Sam Brownes. Neither wears body armor, since they do more running and chasing than shooting. In any case, many police officers and others in law enforcement are well aware that a lot of good cops are now dead because of armored vests, a tragedy that dates back ten years, when a major TV network hysterically generated the cop killer–bullet controversy. Now effectively banned for non-police use, the so-called "cop killer bullet" was made of tungsten carbide, driven at remarkably average velocities to achieve its deep penetration. The round had a sinister green jacket of Teflon, designed to protect an ordnance-steel gun barrel from a harder-than-steel projectile.

No cop, *before* the TV hysteria or *since,* has ever been killed by a bullet designed to be armor-piercing going through his vest. But many officers were shot in the head, neck, armpit and groin by suspects who later admitted that "the cop killer–bullet controversy" had made them aware that cops' torsos might be bulletproof. What armor-piercing bullets didn't do, well-meaning but misinformed anti-gunners did: They caused the deaths of police officers whose vests would otherwise have saved them.

But on April 6, 1991, thirty minutes after midnight, Officers Johnson and Brown had no thoughts of bulletproof vests. It was heading home time, time to look forward to an hour or two of relaxation before hitting the sack.

"What's on TV tonight?" Brown asked. "Anything good?"

Johnson shrugged. "I dunno. Old movies."

"I like old movies," Vernice Brown said. "Humphrey Bogart. James Cagney. Stuff like that. Westerns are good too."

Alan Johnson shrugged. "Whatever turns you on, brother."

They were driving in silence for a while, heading back to headquarters through the quiet, empty streets, when a man who recognized their car suddenly jumped from the side-walk and flagged them down.

Brown rolled his window open and asked, "Hey, what's happening?" He flashed his ever-present smile.

The civilian gulped noisily once or twice, then babbled that a man had hold of a woman down a nearby alley and was raping her. "I think he's holding a gun to her head," he warned. "He's holding the gun and he's raping her at the same time. He has her against a wall."

"The alley was next to an apartment block," Brown says. "We drove down there and got out of the car. I turned to Alan and said, 'Are you gonna get your gun out?' and Alan said, 'Nah, I'm not gonna get my gun out.' Then Alan said, 'Well . . . maybe I'll take my gun out.' And I said, 'Well, let's both take our guns out.'

"It was dark, but we could see the two silhouettes in the alley. We saw by the way the guy's lower body was moving what he was doing. He had his hand on the back of the woman's neck and the gun to her head, and he had her pushed hard up against the wall."

Asked if he then yelled, "Freeze!" Brown laughs and says, "Nah, cops only say that on the TV shows. I can't remember exactly what we said, but I believe Alan yelled, 'Police officers!'"

The rapist was thirty-one-year-old Homer Davis, Jr., an all-round badman with a minor reputation on the streets as a journeyman but ready and willing *pistolero*. Just five days earlier, the massively muscled (more on Davis's impressive physique later, because Officer Brown says the reason for it "burns him up") thirty-one-year-old had been released from a Florida state prison after serving just four years of an eight-year sentence for aggravated assault and kidnapping. The conviction stemmed from an incident in which Davis dragged his former girlfriend from a bus stop at gunpoint and held her in his apartment for a day against her will. She had been holding her three-year-old child while standing at the bus stop with the toddler's father and grandfather. Davis had also at one time or another committed a string of violent crimes, including rape, sexual battery, burglary and threat with a deadly weapon—a bitter legacy that had landed him in jail four times over thirteen years.

When Davis heard Johnson yell, he jumped back and pushed the terrified woman hard toward the two officers. He then snapped off three quick shots from his .38-caliber Charter Arms snubbie.

"I saw the muzzle flashes in the darkness and heard the *blam! blam! blam!* of the gun going off," Brown recalls. "I thought, Oh shit! Here it comes! But the bullets went wide."

Neither officer could return fire at that point, because the woman was between them and Davis.

"If we'd shot back then, we'd have cut her in half," Brown says. "She was right between us and the perp. Then the woman suddenly got clear and Alan fired."

Officer Johnson says he can't recall how many rounds he squeezed off from his big .45—"maybe one, maybe two"— but in any event, he missed clean.

Davis, his smoking piece still at the ready, now legged it to the rear of the alley, where he clambered over a five-foot fence. Johnson went after him.

Shots had been fired, the ball had opened, but Brown waited briefly to make sure the woman stayed put. "I had to secure the witness. We'd shot at a bad guy, and if we couldn't produce the woman who had seen it all, saw Davis fire first, I knew we could get crucified.

"'You say there was a witness to the shooting? Where is this witness?' they'd ask. 'You mean you don't have a witness, Officer Brown? Are you making all this up, Officer Brown?' And so it goes. First thing you have to do in a shooting situation like this is to make sure that the people who saw it stay put."

Like most police officers, Johnson and Brown are keenly aware that there are misguided bleeding hearts throughout our justice system who can, and often do, transform a vicious lowlife like Davis into a holy and devout choirboy who just happened to be quietly standing in an alley, perhaps gazing at the distant stars, pondering the mysteries of the Three Persons in One God, when he was set upon for no reason by a couple of wild-eyed, gun-toting fascists. Hence the priority a streetwise cop places in delaying even a hot chase until the witness is secured and safe. Only then is his own ass secured and safe.

In this case, the officers were lucky. A marked patrol car arrived on the scene and took the terrified victim into protective custody.

Months later, when they were named Police Officers of the Year, Johnson and Brown were credited with saving the young woman's life—Homer Davis, Jr., was not the kind to have left her alive so she could later point the finger at him. In fact, he had spelled this out to his petrified victim during the rape. "After I'm finished, I'm going to kill you," he'd snarled.

There is no doubt whatsoever that at this time both cops could have walked away from the fight heroes, still keeping their honor and reputation intact. In fact many a lawman would have holstered his iron and said, "Ah, the hell with it. It's too dark, and anyhow, Davis knows these alleys and side streets like the back of his hand. No point in getting ambushed and having my head blown off. I'll get the son of a bitch some other day."

But Alan Johnson and Vernice Brown are a different breed of men. Both say that letting Homer Davis go would have been irresponsible and low-down.

"Davis knew we'd recognized him," Brown explains. "And here's what could have easily happened. A few weeks later he's standing on a street corner with a bunch of his buddies, and a rookie cop—and he doesn't know much, this rookie cop—comes strolling toward him.

"Now, maybe the cop only wants to move these guys on from the corner, or maybe he only wants to pass the time of day, but Davis sees him coming and thinks, 'Well, shit, they're on to me.' Then he draws that fast .38 of his and *bang!* there's a dead rookie lying in the gutter and somewhere a wife or a mother will be grieving.

"We couldn't let that happen, even take the slightest chance on that happening. This department has hired around 150 men in the past year to eighteen months, and we have a lot of rookies out there on the street. That's why we had to go after him."

Johnson, as ever more pragmatic, adds: "Besides, the guy had tried to kill us, and that made me madder than hell."

The mark of a good cop is that he knows he must temper his enormous power with responsibility. The mark of a great cop is that he will live up to that responsibility every single day of his service.

Officers Johnson and Brown are such cops.

It takes a long time in the telling, but in fact the decision to go after Davis was made in the split second after Brown saw that his witness was in safe hands.

"After Alan had climbed over the fence, I ran around the side of the building," he says. "I was hoping to cut Davis off before he vanished into the darkness."

Johnson lost the running rapist, who had managed to thumb off a couple of wild rounds during the chase, in the warren of alleys and fences behind the alley. But Brown, coming in from another direction, saw the man running about fifty yards away.

"Alan! I see him," he yelled. "I got him right here."

Brown two-handed his six-inch-barreled Smith and Wesson Model 686 .357-magnum up to eye level and thumbed off a quick shot. The light was bad and it had started to rain, but he saw Davis stagger and fall.

"He's down, Alan!" Brown yelled. "The son of a bitch is down!"

The panting perp had taken a bullet in the leg. But Davis suddenly bounded up, holding his gun high, muzzle skyward, and sprinted past a churchyard. Johnson, running hard, was after him, squeezing off shots as he went.

"Close on him, Vernice!" he yelled. "Cut him off!"

Davis, bleeding badly and gasping frantically for breath, slipped behind a house and climbed onto a fence, where he set up a crude ambush. The rapist had a reputation as a fair hand with a gun, and he lived up to it that night. He'd counted his shots carefully, saving one round. He intended that last round for Alan Johnson.

Johnson, meanwhile, turned the corner of the house and found himself suddenly staring into the muzzle of Davis's .38. The cop was out in the open without cover. But there was a scraggly dandelion growing at his feet, and he ducked behind it—any cover is better than nothing—his .45 coming up fast. He two-handed three very fast shots before his ambusher had a chance to return fire. Two rounds went wide, caroming off into the darkness. The third crashed into Davis's chest, the hollowpoint Hydra-Shok expanding well, ploughing through bone and soft tissue, then destroying a lung. The gunman yelped in pain and terror, then fell backward, thumping heavily into the dirt.

That shot was the last round in Johnson's gun. Later he looked down and saw that the slide of his Smith and Wesson had slammed back out of battery.

"After Alan knocked Davis off the fence, I heard him yelling for me," Brown says. "He had lost his radio during the chase, and we'd communicated by yelling back and forth.

"Davis was dying, but he was still trying to reach his gun,

still trying to get off that one round. I heard Alan say, 'Don't move. Don't reach for the gun.' Davis had lost, and he knew in his last moments of life that he'd lost . . . but he still wanted to take Alan with him.

"When I got there a few seconds later, Homer Davis was already dead.

"By any standard, he was one wicked felon."

Johnson adds: "We got the job done. Homer Davis will never hurt anyone again, never rape another innocent woman. You can believe that."

The entire chase had covered four city blocks. The entire gunfight, from the first shot to the last, had lasted just forty seconds.

In this case credits for gunfighting skills and mental preparedness must go to the police officers. It was dark and rainy, and Davis had fired five times, none of his shots taking effect. The cops fired ten times, making two hits, one of them fatal.

"Some officers, the ones who go in for sports like combat shooting and who are excellent marksmen, might have done better," Brown says. "But in the dark and rain, with the adrenaline pumping, I believe we did about as good as anyone else."

Asked if he'd consciously tried to hit Davis in the leg as the man was running, he says, "I was just trying to hit him. In a gunfight, when your life is on the line, you just try to hit him."

Brown's bullet took the fleeing felon in the calf, but the man's muscles were so huge, so hard, that the devastating .357 slug didn't even slow him down.

"Davis was jailhouse built," Brown says. "He was as tall as Alan but twice as big, and Alan is a real muscular man. All Davis had done in jail for the past four years was to pump iron, getting huge so he could get out and grab a cop."

Cagey, streetwise officers like Johnson and Brown say

that weight rooms should be taken out of our prisons. Many prison gyms are equipped with state-of-the-art machines and free weights, calculated to turn the cons, who have nothing to do but train every single day, into dangerous, colossal clones of Arnold Schwarzenegger. Their progress is carefully monitored by prison experts, and the high-protein prison diet quickly converts into solid muscle.

Meanwhile, the average overworked, underpaid cop, who doesn't have the time or money for fancy gyms, a high-protein diet or a professional weight-training instructor, eats his donuts and drinks his coffee and has to contend with these lethal, predatory behemoths when they get back out on the streets.

"It just doesn't make any sense," Brown says. "Why let these guys pump up in gyms so they can become more efficient criminals and cop killers?"

The gunfight was now over, but unfortunately for Officers Johnson and Brown, the danger was not.

The neighborhood residents spilled, sleepy-eyed, into the street, determined to investigate the late-night gun battle. Within minutes of the last shot, some six hundred people were milling around, and the atmosphere grew tense. It was a familiar South Florida scene: Cops kill an inner-city resident and the street becomes a tinderbox—the slightest spark can ignite an angry explosion of violence, rioting and looting.

"Things did look tense for a while," Brown says. "But the rape victim spoke up, and people who had seen the shooting and some other police officers fanned out through the crowd and kept saying, 'V. and A.J. just shot a man and the circumstances are being investigated.'"

Once the crowd realized what had happened, that Homer Davis was the dead man and that a rape was involved, they calmed down.

"V. and A.J. killed a rapist, that's all," one older man told the people. "It was Homer Davis and he fired first and then he got what he deserved. Now, go home. It's over. It's all over."

The crowd began to disperse, all, that is, except one little banty rooster who seemed particularly aggrieved by the situation and who launched into a tirade against the police to anyone who would listen. But he quickly scampered when Brown, huge, tall and stern, bent down and whispered in his ear: "Chill out man."

When Brown got home that night, strung out and dog tired, he punched a button on his answering machine and heard dozens of messages from concerned residents. One by one, the honest citizens of Pompano Beach were calling to thank him. That's when he finally knew everything was going to be okay.

A few days later, Pompano Police Chief Stanley Tipton received a letter signed by thirty-eight citizens of the neighborhood. It read:

To: Pompano Beach Police.

The incident which took place Sat. which involved officers Brown, Johnson, Relating to the Death of a young man raping a girl. We're sending you this letter of appreciation in handling the situation, very well, and professionally.

So please continue to uphold the law in your "sworn duty" as Pompano's finest.

Thank you.

Of course, there was another side to the coin. The top guns in the neighborhood, or the wannabe top guns, sent out heralds with their challenges: "Come and try to take us. We're a lot better than Homer Davis ever was."

Such is the twisted mentality of the streets.

The honorable courage and dedication to duty of Alan

Johnson and Vernice Brown was rewarded in Minneapolis on October 8, 1991, when the two officers were presented with the Police Officer of the Year Award by the International Association of Chiefs of Police and *Parade* magazine. They later traveled to Washington to help dedicate the National Law Enforcement Officers Memorial.

Chief Tipton, in that stiff-upper-lip, understated style of police chiefs everywhere, said of his men: "We're quite proud of the fact that they continued to pursue, even though they were being shot at."

Today, Officers Johnson and Brown are back on the streets they know so well, still slightly bewildered by their fame, still blinking from the bright glare of their sudden publicity.

They continue to make a living—a painfully modest one—arresting the same folks who once sat next to them in math class.

Most afternoons, right after 4:15 roll call, they might cruise down to the local barbershop and catch up on the neighborhood gossip, then they'll mosey through the back streets, past the small wooden homes where hand-painted signs advertise "YARD SALE" or "CHEAP TVs AND VCRs" or "TIRES." Alan pushes the car past the ball courts where teenage thieves strip cars, or the local Amoco station, which established its place in criminal history when it once made fifteen hundred emergency 911 calls in a single year.

The locals know V. and A.J. well, and the two cops have built up a vast network of sources. They have sharp-eyed spies everywhere who will tip their caps or point a finger when a drug deal is going down.

Since the night of the gunfight, the two men have found a new respect for each other, a respect that goes deep, building on the solid foundation of what had been there before.

Alan says he's had partners in the past who held back on

him when danger threatened. "I'd look around and say, 'Where is that guy?' and see him tiptoeing through the tulips a hundred yards behind me.

"But I always know where Vernice will be. He'll be right there, at my elbow, just where I need him. And he'll be looking straight ahead and he won't be afraid."

If they have a moment to stop and talk about police work, Johnson and Brown will pass on hard-won lessons learned in the tough school of the streets.

"Take backup guns," Brown says. "Some cops carry .38s or .380s as backups. But if you can't get the job done with one gun, having a backup isn't going to help you.

"A lot of times, you're struggling with a perp, and you're both rolling all over the ground, in the dirt, and he's got his hand up your pants leg, rustling around in there, looking for the ankle holster and the backup gun. A cop can get himself killed that way.

"Best thing you can do when you're fighting with a perp, and you're really struggling and he's squawking and kicking and gouging, is to pull your gun out of the holster and throw it away. That way the bad guy can't get at it, and nobody gets badly hurt. When it's just fist to fist, you've a fighting chance of staying alive."

As for the dangers they face daily, Alan Johnson, a father of two, puts it this way: "When you buckle on a gun and put on a badge, you know what you're facing. But you've got a job to do, and no one else is going to do it for you.

"When I get out on the streets, I want to stay alive and go home every day. All I want to do is survive."

"Amen, brother," says Vernice Brown. "Amen."

DEPUTY DON HANSELL

Pershing County,
Nevada, Sheriff's Department

■■■■■■■■■■■■■■■■■■■■

An experienced cop will never use the words "routine traffic stop," because he knows that no traffic stop is ever routine, each has an element of potential danger. The officer who's been around a bit and seen some things will tippytoe around the phrase and end up saying something like "It was a *usual* traffic stop."

Today, that's the way sheriff's deputy Don Hansell says it—after a "routine" traffic stop exploded in his face and ended in blood, terror and blazing gunfire.

Deputy Don Hansell of the Pershing County Sheriff's Department is a man as rugged and enduring as the wild Nevada desert country he patrols in his big, sun-faded Chevy Suburban with the blue bubble-gum machine on top.

A former government hunter and trapper, he reads Louis L'Amour Westerns and in his free time he backpacks into the wild desert country where the Apache once roamed, retracing the steps of those lantern-jawed, laconic L'Amour heroes, men with names like Hondo and Radigan and Shalako.

"If Louis L'Amour writes of a box canyon or an arroyo, it's still there just as he described it, and a man can find it," Hansell says. "He'll talk about a stand of willows beside a creek, and even today you can go there and find the creek and drink the water and camp among the trees.

"He knew every inch of the desert country, and he wrote what he knew."

Louis L'Amour also had a finely honed instinct for recognizing born fighting men, a rare breed, and in this regard he would have heartily approved of Don Hansell.

Hansell stepped over the line that separates men from boys, heroes from the rest of us, in the early morning hours of March 30, 1990, as he drove his Suburban westbound on Interstate 80 toward the town of Lovelock, some ninety miles northeast of Reno.

There are six thousand square miles in Pershing County, most of it mining and cattle country, though seed alfalfa is grown in some of the upper and lower valleys and there are some light industrial plants scattered here and there. Lovelock is the only major town, but this stretch of interstate has a few "white spots," as the cops call them, gas stations mostly, and a scattering of rest stops.

"I was around mile marker 112 or 113 on a regular patrol and I had my CB unit turned on," Hansell says. "The truckers on that stretch of highway are always on the lookout for drunk drivers and such, and they'll get the word to you fast on the CB.

"Then I heard this trucker yell for me. He says, 'Hey, Smokey, look out behind you. You got bear bait comin' up fast behind you. Looks to me like he's drunk.'

"I've been around the Interstate long enough to respect the judgment of the truckers. I knew he was talking about a speeding vehicle, maybe with a drunk driver at the wheel.

"I took my foot off the accelerator and eased my speed down to fifty, maybe fifty-five miles an hour. I kept looking in my rearview mirror, and sure enough I saw headlights come at me, then they swung out and went past me. It was a pickup truck and that thing was flying.

"I figured, 'Well, that's the vehicle,' and I took off after it. He was doing 91 mph on the radar clock as he passed me, then he got into the right-hand slow lane and started to weave a bit. Now I knew I had the right vehicle.

"I got on the radio and told Dispatch that I was about to stop a suspected drunk driver, that I'd followed him for a mile and would pull him over at mile marker 109.

"Dispatch advised me that they'd heard what I'd said, so I went ahead and made a usual traffic stop. I don't want to call it routine, because there ain't no such thing in the dark hours of the early morning when you're miles from any backup."

Hansell walked up to the pickup, a brown 1976 Chevy, California license tag 1J06268, and shone his flashlight into the bed of the truck.

"I had my flashlight in my left hand, and approached the back of the truck real careful," Hansell says. "This is cow country, and sometimes the ranchers carry hunting dogs in the back, and if you get too close, they'll snap at you. The dogs don't mean anything by it; they're just protecting what's theirs.

"Well, there were no dogs in the back of the truck, just boxes and sleeping bags, usual stuff that didn't cause me any great concern. I walked up to the driver's window, and he was just sitting there real still with both hands on the wheel. He had a passenger, and he wasn't moving either."

"I'd like to see your driver's license and your registration, sir," Hansell said. The deputy was tense, alert, but so far had seen nothing to ring his alarm bell, just a man who might or might not have been drunk sitting sheepishly behind the wheel of his truck.

The driver said, "Yeah, well okay, I got them here someplace."

The man then leaned over as if he were going to get the paperwork the deputy had just asked for out of the glove compartment. Hansell took a step forward and lit up the inside of the cab with his flashlight.

"I wanted to see where the guy's hands were going, what he was doing," he says.

"Next thing I know, the guy sits back up and he sticks the muzzle of a .30.30 rifle right at the end of my nose.

"After that, things got real tense in a hurry."

Hansell immediately grabbed the barrel of the rifle. He used the truck door as a fulcrum and levered the barrel downward, trying to break the gunman's grip. But it didn't work. The guy was too strong.

"I thought to myself then, 'Get out of the cone of fire—fast!'" Hansell recalls. "The cone of fire is the area a driver can see out of the door. It starts at the dimensions of the door and spreads outwards, like a big triangle. I was right smack in the middle of it.

"I threw the rifle back in the guy's face as hard as I could, then I turned and ran back towards my patrol unit. I'd taken two, maybe three steps when I heard the rifle go off. I felt the bullet slam into my back. It seemed like it hit me right on the spine, under the bottom edge of my vest armor and just above my gunbelt. The force of the bullet knocked me flat on my face in front of the Suburban. I remember thinking, 'Oh shit, I'm lying right in the middle of my own headlights.'"

The dazed deputy reached up and grabbed the mike of his personal radio from a loop on the upper right side of his bulletproof vest and yelled, "Shots fired. Officer down. I've been hit and I need help."

"I don't know how I got there, but I found myself turned around, so that I was looking out over my feet at the gunman's vehicle," Hansell says. "I saw the driver's door open. I watched the guy get out and he levered another .30.30 shell into the chamber of his rifle. It was a Marlin Model 336, a real nice side-ejection deer rifle.

"The guy with the rifle came toward me, and I raised my Coonan .357-magnum semi-automatic and fired the entire seven-round magazine of Winchester 125-grain jacketed hollowpoints at him. I was scared, real scared, and I didn't try to aim the piece. I just leveled the weapon and cut loose.

"After I dumped the seven rounds in his direction, the guy with the rifle scuttled back into the truck and slammed the door after him."

So far, Hansell was still alive for a number of reasons. For one thing he was full of spit and vinegar and still very much in the fight. Secondly, his sidearm, the reliable, American-made Coonan Arms .357-magnum, is one of the world's great fighting handguns. And thirdly, his training and mental conditioning allowed him to use his handgun tactically, turning a basically defensive weapon into an offensive one, so that he *attacked* his attacker.

The deputy's training had also helped him overcome the third automatic response mechanism that kicks in when an individual is confronted at close range by a deadly, violent attack. The first two are Fight or Flight. The third is . . . Do Nothing. This is a shock-induced inertia, a mental paralysis that leaves someone completely unable to act. It is caused entirely by a lack of training, and over the years it has left many a good cop dead on the ground.

"After I saw the guy disappear into his truck, I dropped the clip from the Coonan and slammed in another one," Hansell says. "I was lying in my headlights, and I tried to move out of there, but I couldn't. I had no feeling in my legs from the waist down, and I couldn't move them.

"I didn't need anyone to tell me that I was in one hell of a fix.

"I looked up and saw the rifle, with two hands holding it, poke out of the window of the pickup. The guy triggered a shot, and the radiator of the Suburban exploded, and the hot steam with the antifreeze came hissing out. I'll never forget that smell, the smell you get from hot antifreeze oozing out of a busted radiator.

"My Coonan came up again, and I fired three fast shots at the guy with the rifle, and he ducked back inside his truck.

"Once again I grabbed my chest mike and yelled for help.

This time my dispatcher, Joanne Graham, came back to me. 'They're on the way,' she said.

"Headquarters is about two miles from where I was lying at mile marker 109, so I reckoned help would arrive soon. Meantime I looked up, and the guy in the pickup is taking aim again. This time the left front tire of the patrol unit exploded, and again I snapped off a few fast shots, forcing him back inside.

"I was lying there in the glare of my headlights, my legs paralyzed, and I couldn't hear a siren, couldn't see headlights, just that damn pickup truck in front of me. I thought I must have been lying there for hours. I kept saying over and over, 'Come on, guys, get here. Get here.'"

The rifleman in the truck fired again. This time the bullet *whaaanged!* spitefully off the asphalt close to the deputy's head.

"I was with the 173rd Airborne in Vietnam, mostly in ambush and recon, and in the thirteen months I was there I'd heard enough ricocheting bullets to know when they are close," Hansell says. "And that one was close. I fired again, two or three shots, and again I drove the guy back into his truck.

"The gun has to be dry, I thought, so I dropped the clip and slapped in another one. When I looked up again, the pickup was pulling away from me, real slow.

"'You sons of bitches, you're not gonna leave me laying here!' I yelled, and I kinda rolled over on my right side and loosed off my third clip at them. I have to admit that I was fighting mad. The pickup was about thirty yards from me and picking up speed, and I was still blazing away at it."

Excellent loads that they are, the Winchester 125-grain JHPs still failed to penetrate the cab of the truck—though all of Hansell's twenty-one rounds hit the vehicle.

"I lay there after the truck had gone and thought to myself: 'Well, you're still alive, Don. You're gonna make it,'" Hansell recalls.

"I still didn't know where my guys were, and figured I'd been lying there for hours. I kept saying, 'Why don't they come? Why don't they come?'"

Later, by checking the times of Hansell's calls to Dispatch, his department calculated that one minute and forty-five seconds elapsed between his first call for help to the arrival of backup units.

The deputy says that he was completely paralyzed from the waist down, but had no pain. "It was like somebody had cut my body in half and thrown the legs away," he says.

As he lay there, Hansell looked around and saw the tall, burly figure of a man walking toward him.

"It was real dark, and this guy looked like the driver of the pickup," he says. "I thought to myself, 'Dammit, he's coming back to get me.'

"I laid the Coonan on him and said, 'If you take one more step, I'm gonna drop you dead on the ground.'

"The guy spread his hands and said, 'Hey, I'm a truck driver and I seen what happened. I'm here to help you.'

"I said, 'Just don't move. If you come at me, I'm gonna shoot you down. I got deputies coming and I'll trust them. I don't know you and I'm not gonna trust you.'

"That's what I told him, and the guy stopped where he was. He didn't move a muscle after that."

Later Hansell learned that the trucker had seen the gunfight and had bravely tried to stop the fleeing pickup with his eighteen-wheeler. He'd attempted to sideswipe the bullet-pocked Chevy with his less-than-nimble vehicle—and missed.

Moments after the Good Samaritan trucker froze in his tracks (and who can blame him?) the backup units arrived and Hansell found himself trying to focus on the deeply concerned faces of his fellow deputies and jailer Rick Mathues.

"Rick pointed to the trucker and said, 'Is this him? Is this guy the one?' I shook my head and said I didn't know. The shock was getting to me, and I was starting to drift in and out of consciousness. Then I recall this ambulance guy and he's saying to me, 'Stay awake! You gotta stay awake!' "

Hansell was taken by helicopter to a Reno hospital. "I don't remember the ride," he says. "But I recall waking up when the chopper landed and then seeing these bright hospital corridor lights whizzing past my face. Somebody in a white coat asked me something and I blacked out.

"I woke up fourteen days later."

As Hansell was being rushed to the hospital, police, sheriff and Highway Patrol units were converging on the area from all over Pershing and neighboring counties.

Lovelock Highway Patrolman Sandy Smith, driving a Ford Mustang, spotted the fugitive pickup and gave chase at speeds that often exceeded 120 mph. He saw the truck leave the highway and take off across a gravel pit, and he followed, only to bog down when his vehicle ran out of gas.

Smith saw the pickup get back on the freeway around mile marker 83, and he lit out after it.

"I'm in close pursuit," Smith radioed headquarters. "The suspect truck is back on the freeway, heading south."

Minutes later Smith looked down at his gauges and groaned—his Mustang, burning up fuel because of the high-speed chase, was also running out of gas. Smith pulled over and got on his radio to patrol units in the town of Fernly, some forty miles away. He was told that Fernly Highway Patrol units were now in pursuit of the suspect vehicle, which was heading back toward Lovelock and was currently passing mile marker 72. But the pickup suddenly swung off the freeway, crashed through the right-of-way barrier and took off across the desert, heading for the hills. The Highway Patrol cars, all of them two-wheel-drive sedans and useless in the desert, pulled over, and the officers watched helplessly as the pickup vanished into the night.

"Well, shit," one patrolman groaned. "We'll never catch them now, not in the desert."

But within minutes a forty-mile stretch of freeway, from mile marker 83 to Fernly, was closed to all traffic, and four-wheel-drive units began to fan out across the pitch blackness of the desert. Eventually there were sixty men on the ground, including dog handlers and a crack heavy-weapons SWAT team from Reno.

The searchers found the pickup abandoned about three miles from the freeway. The vehicle had been stripped and the license plate taken off, and the stuff that had been in the bed was gone.

Two sets of tracks led away from the truck toward a plant that made kitty litter from the diatomaceous earth that abounded in the desert. The SWAT team went into the plant and found nothing.

Within minutes another search team picked up the tracks again, this time heading into the desert, only to lose them in some scattered rocks.

"We're getting nowhere fast," a senior officer said. "We better lay low till sunup and then resume the search. You boys just stretch out and relax till then."

It was still just four in the morning, and the night was cool, moonless and dark, so the cops called off the search till daylight, when the Highway Patrol could get a plane in the air and the local Fish and Game people could send up their helicopter.

At first light, as the two aircraft began their search patterns, one of the dog handlers picked up the tracks again. The man followed them for a few hundred yards, then very quickly retraced his steps. He called out to Deputy Bill Barks and pointed to the tracks angling out into the desert.

"I saw those tracks go out into the desert and then they just stopped," the man said. "I mean, you look out across the sand and the tracks stop dead, like the men making them disappeared off the face of the earth."

The desert at that point is level sand covered by sagebrush. There's nothing for miles around that grows more than twelve inches high.

"Nobody disappears into thin air," said the vigilant Barks. The big deputy pulled his gun and followed the two pairs of footprints, and sure enough the tracks came to a sudden stop.

The deputy looked around and saw nothing, then he happened to glance at a bush beside his feet—and saw two bloodshot eyeballs peering up at him through the sand. The fugitives had buried themselves in the ground and pulled sagebrush around them.

Barks says he "became unglued" because he couldn't locate the rifle and feared the fugitives might be holding it in instant readiness. The deputy knew he had to act quickly. He bent over, jammed the muzzle of his gun between the eyeballs at his feet and said quietly: "Even blink, an' I'll scatter your fucking brains."

Moments later he was prodding his two crestfallen prisoners ahead of him toward the other members of the search party.

"I think I've found what we've been looking for," Barks said.

The rifleman who had shot Deputy Hansell was Carlos Anthony Bryand, a Mexican male aged twenty-one. His buddy was Erwin Eugene Enders, a Caucasian aged twenty. Both were from California, out of the San Jose area.

Bryand was later bound over in the district court on charges of attempted murder with a deadly weapon, conspiracy to commit murder, resisting an officer and discharging a firearm into a vehicle.

Enders, who had apparently done nothing but lie on the floor of the pickup during the encounter, was charged with conspiracy to commit murder and resisting a public officer.

At their trial before Judge Llewellyn Young, Enders said, "When we drove past the deputy's truck, Carlos turned to me and said, 'Are you afraid to die?' I told him I wasn't and asked why he'd asked me that. He answered, 'Because if that cop stops me, I'm gonna shoot him.'"

Bryand was found guilty on all four counts and sentenced to fifty-eight years imprisonment. Enders was given six years and fined five thousand dollars.

In all, Bryand fired seven shots at Hansell, and one of the factors that saved the deputy's life was the white dome of his radar set sticking up over the dashboard of the Suburban. At one point Bryand fired several rounds at it, thinking the deputy had somehow gotten back into his vehicle and that the dome was his head.

The only bullet that hit the deputy was the one that slammed into his back as, bent over, he ran from the pickup truck. The heavy .30.30 round entered Hansell's back an inch-and-a-half to the right of his spine at gunbelt level. It exited four inches to the right of his navel, struck the inside of his armored vest and dropped to the ground.

During his time in Reno's Washoe Med Hospital, Hansell had major surgery twice to repair the terrible damage to his stomach and other organs.

His doctors found him a less than cooperative patient.

When Hansell woke up after fourteen days of unconsciousness, he asked his doctor, "Okay, can I go home now?"

The surgeon shook his head and said, "You're not going anywhere for a while yet. You're shot through and through."

"Hell, Doc, I know that," Hansell replied. "I only gotta lift the sheet to see the holes."

Hansell was determined to get out of bed and asked for crutches, which were flatly refused. "In your state, you could barely crawl, let alone walk," his physician told him.

Finally, after a great deal of wheedling, the long-suffering doctor gave in. "When you can walk around your room on crutches, you can go home," he said.

Hansell smiled. Three days later he walked around his room. Then he went home.

"I just never could abide hospitals," he says.

Today Deputy Hansell is back on duty. He has permanent nerve damage to his right leg and has no feeling on the outside of his thigh from his hip to his knee.

There is one part of the shoot-out and subsequent manhunt that is still a mystery—where did the boxes and sleeping bags from the back of the pickup go?

"After I was able to walk and move around better, I took my four-wheel-drive out into the desert to look for them," Hansell says. "But I never did find them.

"I think it's a real possibility that the orange and apple boxes in the back of the truck held drugs."

Hansell says his wife Frances is "a very religious woman" and wants him to get out of the law enforcement business.

"She just doesn't like this line of work," Hansell says. "My son and daughter don't mind so much. They know I can take care of myself.

"I still like to get out in the desert with my Louis L'Amour books, and my wife and I still go deer hunting, though I drive her crazy most of the time when we're out there.

"Frances is a meat hunter. She wants a deer in the freezer for the wintertime. Me, I'm a trophy hunter, that's why I've only killed two bucks in twenty-six years of hunting. I used to hunt with a rifle, and figured that was too easy. Then I switched to a handgun, and that got too easy. Now I use a bow and arrow, and it's almost impossible to hit anything. If my family was depending on me to bring home meat, we'd all be kinda lank in the flank by this time.

"Most of the time, even after stalking for hours, I just lay my bow aside and watch the does, they're such beautiful animals. Sometimes that's when my wife gets mad at me, telling me there's no meat in the freezer.

"But I don't mind. I'm out there in the desert country I love and I'm just glad to be alive."

In the Line of Duty . . .

Patrolman James Wier
Denver, Colorado, Police Department

■■■■■■■■■■■■■■■■■■■■■■

On June 3, 1987, Shawn Marie Wier sat in front of her TV breastfeeding her baby son. She had just tuned in to the ten o'clock news. Two minutes later her world fell apart, and nothing in her life would ever be the same again.

A grim-faced anchorman reported that two police officers had just been shot in Denver. Then the man's voice was garbled by static and Shawn couldn't hear the names of the officers.

But she knew.

She knew with all of her woman's intuition that the incident had happened in the sector where her husband was on duty.

Then the phone rang. And rang. And rang.

"I walked out into the kitchen and I just stared at the telephone," Shawn says. "But finally I moved my hand and made myself answer it."

A man's voice, hard-edged with stress, said, "Is this Mrs. Wier?"

"Yes."

"Is this Officer James Wier's mother?"

"No, it's his wife."

"Did you hear about the shooting?"

51

"Oh my God . . . was it Jim?"

"He's in the emergency room."

Shawn Wier was seventy miles from Denver. It would take her at least an hour to reach the hospital. As she prepared to leave, her eyes were drawn back to the TV screen. She saw her husband lying on a stretcher, being carried from an ambulance. There was an oxygen mask over Jim's mouth, but his long legs hung limply over the end of the stretcher.

"He's dead," Shawn whispered.

When she arrived at the hospital, Jim's mother and brother were already there. She didn't have to ask. Their faces told her everything she needed to know.

"I want to see him," Shawn said. "I want to hold his hand one last time."

They took her to the cold morgue and pulled Jim out of a steel drawer. They had put brown lunch bags over his hands for prints and powder residue.

"I couldn't touch his hands," Shawn recalls. "I couldn't hold them.

"After that I went on automatic pilot. You have to."

Jim Wier and his wife were both twenty-five years old. They had been married less than a year. Their son Dustin had been born just five weeks before. Their other son Dirk was three.

Officer Wier was killed by a deranged cop-hater named Charles Tarr, a man who flew the American flag upside down and equated the Denver Police Department with the KGB.

On the night Officer Wier died, Tarr had made yet another of his many harassing crank calls to the police. A few minutes later his wife Mary called, and told the dispatcher to ignore her husband, that he was drunk. But the dispatcher then heard a scuffle and Tarr yelling at his wife. Fearing for the woman's safety, he sent Patrolmen James Wier and

Jimmy Gose to the house at 40 S. Pennsylvania Street. When the two officers arrived they saw a man behind the screen door with a rifle or a shotgun in his hands.

What the two officers didn't know was that the mentally unbalanced Tarr was prepared to die that night—and he wanted to take a cop with him.

As the patrolmen dived for cover, Tarr cut loose with his rifle. As James Wier rose up from behind a three-foot stucco wall to return fire, Tarr shot him in the head. Before the gunfight ended, two more officers were wounded. Tarr then killed himself with his own gun.

"The last memory I have of Jim is from the afternoon of the day he died," Shawn says. "We were having a picnic in the backyard and it started to hail. Jim and I just stood there, with the hail coming down, laughing and kissing each other.

"Before Jim died, I felt safe, secure and happy. I want that back."

In the months and years that followed, Shawn Wier slowly put the shattered fragments of her life back together again. She completed a Master's degree in Communications, and on October 13, 1989, became the wife of another police officer, Patrick O'Conner of the New York City Police Department.

"I was very lucky to find this wonderful man," she says. "But the pain of Jim's death is not over . . . and it never will be."

Officer O'Conner can understand what Shawn's been through. His father, one of New York's finest, was killed in the line of duty in November 1973.

Shawn says she doesn't worry about her husband's safety. She explains: "Pat always says, 'If you worry, you're going to die. If you don't worry, you're still going to die.' I try to remember that."

Shawn Wier has started to build a new life, and the deep wounds of the past are slowly healing. But she will never forget James Wier and the love she felt for him. She tells her sons about him often, letting them know what a fine man he was and how he once stood in a hailstorm and laughed.

She doesn't want her sons to forget him either.

OFFICER STACY LIM
Los Angeles Police Department

■■■■■■■■■■■■■■■■■■■■■■

It was the wee, small hours in Los Angeles, but the city was not quiet. Early morning revelers still thronged the downtown bars and nightclubs, wading through the reflections of the neon lights splashed on the sidewalks like spilled paint, congregating under the flashing Miller Lite signs before going inside to join the smoky clamor of the Friday night late crowd. Cars full of laughing, carefree teenagers cruised the Strip, their expensive Motorolas, dull yellow-green rectangles on cluttered dashboards, blasting heavy metal from four, six or even eight speakers, tuned to the A.M. deejays who spun the compacts and were "makin' with the flak, Jack, so keep outta the sack," promising between platters that the clear, dry weather would continue at least through the weekend and that the surf was lookin' good. "Hey, we're talkin' quality beach time here, folks, guys, gals an' pals, so get out there an' enjoy!"

In the distance, the downtown crowd might have heard the sudden screech of police and ambulance sirens being drawn across the black chalkboard of the night like ragged fingernails. But if the solidly middle- and upper-class teenagers in their Mustang, Mazda and Mercedes convertibles took any notice it was only to shake their golden heads

and briefly tell themselves, perhaps thankfully, that the
sirens had nothing to do with them. That was the primal wail
of another world out there in the caverns of darkness beyond
the downtown lights, the surreal, dangerous world of cops,
victims . . . and predators.

They also had no way of knowing that for a young police
officer named Stacy Lim, who was at that moment lying in
a suburban driveway, her heart torn apart by a bullet, the
sirens heralded the end of one battle for life . . . and the
beginning of another . . .

A city like Los Angeles is the natural habitat and hunting
ground of the predator, and the darkness is his friend. It is a
black cloak thrown over the canyons of his streets and
alleys, under which he can scuttle and scurry and whisper
and stalk.

Normally, a fit, young police officer has little to fear from
a predator—though, like a rat, the predator will fight if
cornered, often savagely. No, his natural prey is the weak,
the sick, the aged and the infirm, not the strong in body, well
practiced in the use of arms. In nature the predator plays a
useful role, ensuring the survival of only the fittest, thus
improving by his predation the breeding stock. But in the
modern city the predator fulfills no such function. He brings
only terror, pain and sudden, shrieking death.

So it was during the early morning hours of June 9, 1990,
that a predator pack sighted a slight, young Oriental woman
driving a 1988 Ford Bronco II on the Golden State Freeway.

It was 1:30 A.M. and off-duty LAPD Officer Stacy Lim,
twenty-seven, was returning to her home in the Canyon
Country after having dropped off her vacation requests for
the next month at the Northeast Division police station.

Stacy was feeling pretty good that night. Earlier in the
evening the five-foot-seven, 110-pound officer had played
softball for her coed team, the Jus Cuz, and had then gone

to a teammate's home to hang out, eat popcorn and watch a movie on the VCR.

She left after midnight, still dressed in her softball uniform, then dropped off her vacation form at the station before making her way home.

She didn't know it then, but the predators had picked up the scent and begun their stalk . . . which was to cover a distance of thirty miles.

There were five of them in the pack, all gang members, two juvenile males, two juvenile females and an adult male who was driving their car.

The psychologists tell us that young people like these become the way they are because of a whole set of complex social problems for which the public at large is mostly to blame.

"Just beat your breast, say mea culpa, and give them what they want, and they'll be as right as rain," we're told.

Maybe that is so. But what they wanted that night was Stacy Lim's car with its custom wheel rims, and they were quite prepared to kill her to get it. What they didn't know was that the young officer wasn't about to beat her breast and part with her treasured blue Bronco without a struggle.

In fact, one of the juveniles told detectives later, "We wanted those wheel rims, but if we'd known she was a cop, we wouldn't have tried to take them.

"Hey, man, we thought she was just some dumb chick out late on the road after leaving her boyfriend. We thought she'd be real easy."

According to a report issued by the LAPD, the adult gang member, Arvin Peter Mani, twenty, dropped off sixteen-year-old Joel Valenzuela and a thirteen-year-old female at the corner of Nadel Street, a few yards from Stacy's home.

"Go get her," Mani said. "Just get the fuckin' Bronco and don't take no shit. Know what I mean?"

Valenzuela grinned at Mani as he stepped out of the car,

his fingers lightly tapping the walnut grips of the .357-magnum revolver in the waistband of his jeans.

Mani then slowly drove past the police officer's car and braked to a stop a few yards away.

The police learned later that the plan was for Valenzuela and the girl to steal the Bronco, then follow the other car back into the dark canyons of the city, where it would be stripped and sold as parts.

It is obvious that the strong, husky Valenzuela took slender Stacy Lim for an easy mark—a mistake that within a few seconds would cost him his life in a sudden, lethal blaze of gunfire.

"Valenzuela and the girl approached me as I was getting out of my car," Stacy remembers.

"I always keep my service pistol under my right thigh when I drive, and as I got out of the Bronco, I held it hidden behind my leg. If these were just two innocent kids, maybe looking for directions, I didn't want to scare them to death by showing my weapon."

The young cop identified herself as a police officer and was about to ask Valenzuela, who was naked from the waist up, what he wanted. Then she saw the gun.

"It was pointed right at my chest from a distance of about three feet," she says. "All I saw was that gun. I had tunnel vision that night. I don't remember looking at Valenzuela . . . just that gun, which looked enormous, stuck right in my face . . ."

Then came "a thunderous noise" and a bright light like a flashbulb going off, and Stacy Lim felt "like a sharpened iron bar, heated white hot, had been driven clean through my chest."

Valenzuela, with the gang-member breed's customary disregard for human life, had fired a .357-magnum bullet, no questions asked, at point-blank range, into the officer's heart.

Stacy says the impact of the high-velocity slug slammed her back against the open door of her car. But in this, she is in error. Despite what we see in the movies or on TV, of people being blasted backward—often spectacularly crashing through plate glass windows—by the force of a bullet, no handgun round is powerful enough to knock someone off their feet. The body absorbs the bullet's impact and closes around the temporary wound cavity like gelatin, so the body itself acts as a shock absorber.

What is more likely is that the slender young cop staggered backward from pain, shock and surprise and fell against the door of her Bronco.

She didn't learn until much later that Valenzuela's bullet had blown a hole through the base of her heart, then fragmented, drilling into her spleen, liver and large and small intestines, finally rupturing a major artery and breaking a rib as it exited her back, leaving an exit hole the size of a tennis ball. Stacy was still on her feet, still thinking, still in the fight, but she was already suffering the massive internal bleeding that would almost cost her life.

With a courage and determination that is truly incredible, the critically injured officer brought up her Beretta 92F service pistol and fired one round at Valenzuela. The official police-issue, 9mm Federal 125-grain jacketed hollowpoint struck the gunman in the chest and halted his attack. He then turned and ran to the rear of Stacy's Bronco, a distance of about twelve feet.

It should be noted here that the high-capacity 9mm semi-automatic pistol is like the Great White shark—it is simply a killing machine, and the big Beretta 92F, which is the new service pistol of our armed forces, is one of the best of the breed.

But like all handguns, it is a defensive, not an offensive, weapon. One-shot kills are very rare in gunfights where the antagonists are armed with handguns, and the most that can be expected of any handgun is that it will incapacitate or injure the aggressor badly enough so that he will break off his attack.

In Stacy Lim's case, her service Beretta performed this function admirably.

At this point Valenzuela was probably also in shock, both from his gunshot wound and the immediate, awful realization that his "easy mark," this weak, helpless victim, had suddenly grown claws and fangs.

Stacy chased her attacker as he ran to the rear of the Bronco. She saw him stop, turn and face her again, his .357 revolver coming up fast.

The young cop's first shot had been fired double action, meaning that with one long pull of the trigger she'd brought the hammer back and then let it fall on the firing pin. Now the Beretta had reverted to single-action mode. The trigger pull was consequently shorter and lighter, because the hammer of the gun cocked itself between shots due to the return action of the slide.

Stacy fired three times with amazing speed and skill, scoring with all three rounds, and Valenzuela dropped. He was probably already dead when he hit the ground. The young officer then ran into the street.

"At that point I didn't know how many attackers there were and from which direction they might be coming from," she says. "This time I wanted to be prepared if they came at me again."

But Nadel Street was empty . . . Mani and the other juveniles had fled at the first whiff of gunsmoke.

Bleeding, in great pain and losing consciousness fast, Stacy Lim staggered up the driveway of her modest stucco home—and collapsed.

From the first shot to the last, the gunfight had lasted about five seconds.

One of Stacy's roommates rushed out of the house and

found her friend unconscious, the blood forming a dark red pool around the officer's body.

"Stacy!" the girl screamed. "Stacy, for God's sake what happened?"

The young woman put her arm under Stacy's shoulders, lifting her head gently from the concrete driveway. Then she looked down at the front of her nightdress and saw that it was already stained deep red with blood.

"Oh my God," the stunned woman whispered. She gently laid her friend's head back on the hard concrete and rushed inside. The woman frantically dialed 911 . . . and within minutes the sirens began.

Flanked by an escort of four wailing police cars, Stacy's ambulance rushed her to Henry Mayo Hospital in nearby Newhall, where she was immediately prepared for emergency surgery.

One of the escorting cops, a fresh-faced kid in his early twenties, caught one of the rushing doctors by the arm. "Does . . . does she have a chance, Doc?" he asked.

The doctor shook his head. "It's bad," he said. "Real bad."

Meanwhile the body of Valenzuela still lay in the street, his fallen .357 close to his stiffening hand. The half-naked corpse would lie there, ignored, for several hours while neighbors gawked and pointed and shook their heads and the investigating officers constantly stepped around and over it.

Like many of his kind, the teenager had died a death more fitting a mad dog than a human being. But his death had been of his own choosing, and the handgun had written his epitaph in blood.

The thirteen-year-old girl who had been with Valenzuela had run down the street after the shooting and hidden in some bushes. She was found by deputies who were searching nearby yards.

"She seemed calm. She wasn't even crying," says a

teenage boy who lives on Nadel Street. "It was as if nothing had happened. Her boyfriend's death and the wounded cop didn't mean a thing to her. She looked bored by the whole thing."

Other witnesses said that the girl looked at Valenzuela's body as if it were a "dead dog lying there. She was totally without emotion. Uncaring."

Los Angeles Police Chief Daryl F. Gates, three deputy chiefs, various commanders and at least one police commissioner surveyed the scene of the attack, then rushed to the hospital.

When the police bosses arrived, twenty members of Stacy's softball team were already there . . . and the young cop's parents were getting some bad news.

A grim-faced surgeon gently tried to prepare the couple for the worst. "I have to tell you," he said. "Stacy is hurt bad. Real bad. I don't think she's going to make it. Her heart was hit and she's lost massive amounts of blood. I wish I had better news. I don't think I can even give you some hope."

"Not even that?" the young cop's father asked.

"Not even that," the doctor said.

As is usual in cases where cops are shot in the line of duty, the hospital quickly filled up with anxious friends and relatives. Next to arrive was Stacy's brother, Deputy Christian Lim of the Los Angeles County Sheriff's Department, followed by more members of the softball team. Anxious off-duty police colleagues kept showing up throughout the long morning, till more than two hundred people had crowded into the waiting room.

When Stacy entered the emergency room, she was to all intents and purposes already dead. She had no vital signs. One of the emergency room doctors pumped her shattered heart with his bare hands for forty-five minutes, finally getting a faint beat. A full surgical team, including one of our nation's top heart specialists, then worked for several hours to repair the extensive damage to Stacy's body, feverishly trying to stop the massive internal hemorrhaging. At one point during this superhuman effort on the part of the surgical team, Stacy's vital signs stopped again.

"We've lost her," one of the doctors said.

Electrical shock pads were laid on the young cop's chest, and her body arched convulsively as the current jolted again and again through her heart. Within a few seconds a faint heartbeat fluttered weakly through the monitor, and the job of repairing the punctures in her internal organs continued.

After surgery Stacy was taken to Intensive Care, but the internal bleeding would not stop. During the next few hours she was to receive a total of 101 units of blood, all of it donated by friends and fellow officers.

But it seemed that the efforts of the surgeons were to be all in vain. Stacy went into full cardiac arrest and was once again rushed into the operating room. The doctors removed her heart from her chest cavity and massaged the damaged organ till her heartbeat once again showed a flutter of activity on the monitor.

The surgeons still thought there was little chance that the young woman would survive.

Again, her parents were told, "Your daughter has about two hours, maybe less, to live. Perhaps it's better that you make your preparations now. If there is a clergyman . . ."

But Stacy's friends and fellow officers were not about to give up that easily. Cops in uniform, friends still in nightgowns crowded around the dying woman's bed and urged: "Come on, Stacy, don't give up now. You can make it . . . you can make it . . . you can make it . . ."

Then a miracle happened.

Stacy Lim moved her right index finger upward about half an inch. She was letting everyone know that she could hear, that she was fighting back.

One of the off-duty cops rushed outside and found a doctor, telling the amazed surgeon that Stacy was conscious.

"Get in there, Doctor," the cop said. "She's fighting back. She's going to make it. I just know she is."

The physician said later: "Something happened in that room which we don't understand. Stacy Lim should have died right there in Intensive Care. We had done all we could for her and believed that her finger had moved because of all the heart stimulant drugs she'd been given. But as the next few hours showed, she was indeed growing steadily stronger. There was no doubt about it . . . she was fighting back."

The assembled reporters tried to get a statement from the watch commander of the Northeast Division, Stacy's superior officer. But a uniformed cop came out of the man's office and said simply, "He can't talk. He has tears in his eyes. He is so emotional. This just isn't the time, ladies and gentlemen. Maybe later, huh? Maybe a little later."

However Lieutenant Dave Waterman, Stacy's supervisor on the evening shift, when asked for a statement, told the media: "In the six months she's been here in the Northeast Division, Stacy Lim has proved to be a fine officer who has earned the respect and affection of her colleagues."

Asked if she excelled at any particular aspect of police work, Waterman replied, "Right now, Officer Lim excels at surviving."

And survive she did.

After ten days in Intensive Care, the young woman who since childhood had always wanted to be a cop, was moved to a regular hospital room. Then, on June 26, seventeen days after she'd been shot through the heart, Stacy Lim left the hospital. She did not use a wheelchair. She walked.

She returned to full police duty eight months later.

"I didn't want a desk job; I wanted back out on the street," she says. "I feel that I'm putting something worthwhile into this community, and doing the job I always wanted to do.

"I was not about to let some punk with a gun change all that. If I had refused to go back on street duty, I would have lost and he would have been the winner."

Today, Stacy Lim still plays softball, for a police team, still goes to a friend's house after the game to eat popcorn and watch a movie, still drives her treasured Bronco.

"I guess I survived because it wasn't my time to go," she says. "God must still have plans for me down here."

If you ask her how she managed to recover from her terrible wounds, she'll tell you that it was the prayers and support of her friends and fellow officers that helped pull her through.

And she'll smile and add one thing more: "I'm also a fighter."

On July 19 San Fernando Superior Court Judge John H. Major sentenced Arvin Peter Mani to ten years for his part in the attack on Stacy Lim. This is the maximum term for attempted second-degree murder, one of two charges to which he pleaded guilty after prosecutors dropped three other counts.

Judge Major said that even though Officer Lim was shot by another of the four alleged participants, he gave the maximum sentence because Mani had masterminded the robbery attempt—the third one the gang had attempted that night.

"Mr. Mani is the fellow who took these young people on this hunt to find somebody to do something to, and they did it," Major said.

"They looked around in Highland Park and didn't find anything they'd like to steal, and they saw this victim who is alive today because of some miracle."

Mani also pleaded guilty to a count of conspiracy to commit robbery, to which he was sentenced to one year, which he now serves concurrently with his longer sentence.

The District Attorney's Office had also filed a count of attempted first-degree murder against Mani, but reduced it to second-degree murder because it could not be proven that he intended to kill the young officer.

Two girls, aged thirteen and fourteen, were later dealt with in Central Juvenile Court on charges of attempted murder, conspiracy to commit robbery, attempted grand theft auto and assault with a firearm. An eleven-year-old accomplice was released without charges.

Mani's attorney, Deputy Public Defender Alan Budde, had asked the court for leniency because his client had a clean record and felt "remorse" over the shooting.

According to court records, Mani sent Stacy Lim a letter after the shooting in which he wrote:

"Get well soon. I hope you are feeling better. I am sincerely sorry for what happened to you. I know you must have gone through torture and hell, just like I am now.

"I never thought anything like this could happen to me or anybody . . ."

She never answered it.

■   ■   ■

Stacy Lim was later honored as Officer of the Year by the American Police Hall of Fame. Gerald Arenberg, executive director of the National Association of Chiefs of Police, said at the time: "Stacy Lim is one of the gutsiest police officers I have ever met, male or female. Her valor and courage are an inspiring example for others to follow."

OFFICER KENNETH MORSETTE AND CAPTAIN MIKE CONNELLY
Indian Police, Blackfeet Reservation, Browning, Montana

■ ■

The Indian police have a 120-year tradition of honorable service and valor that dates back to their part in the capture of the great Apache war chief Geronimo in the 1870s, and continues unabated to the present day.

Native American officers first gained a reputation for dedication to duty and personal gallantry during the wild days of the 1870s, when they helped the U.S. cavalry track down rampaging Apache renegades, and later, at the turn of the century, when men like the peerless Sam Sixkiller used the Colt revolver and Winchester rifle to end illicit liquor traffic in the Indian territories.

Today, within the confines of the emotionally charged and sometimes explosively violent tribal reservations, the men and women of the Indian police continue that honorable tradition. They work under extremely difficult conditions, not least of which is chronic underfunding by a parsimonious government. This lack of money often shows up in shortages of necessary law enforcement items like spark plugs, tires and efficient car radios, and more seriously, in a lack of manpower that can put an officer's nearest backup as many as eighty miles away.

No wonder that many a long-serving Indian cop will talk

wistfully about some of the tax-supported and well-heeled big-city departments, and sigh: "Now if we only had that kind of funding, we could do wonders out here."

But the Indian officer is long-practiced in making do with what he has, and continues to improve the quality and efficiency of his work to better safeguard the communities he is sworn to protect.

In the days before the white man came, the failure of a tribal police society to carry out its sacred duty would have meant the failure of the hunt for the whole tribe and raised the prospect of starvation.

In the 1990s, the strength and health of the Indian communities is no less dependent on the maintenance of safety and justice by their law enforcement officers and the Indian judges who administer their courts.

The traditional gallantry of the Indian police is unquestioned. But even so, it comes as a surprise to find two officers, both within the same small department, who hold the coveted Medal of Valor. The acts of bravery of these men were very different. Yet taken together they illustrate the very real dangers Native American officers face—often on a daily basis—and the reserves of courage they are forced to call upon so often that valorous deeds become commonplace, and the way of the hero becomes routine.

Kenneth Morsette is a Gros Ventre Indian and a police officer on the Blackfeet reservation in Browning, Montana. He is a five-foot-four-inch, 205-pound tank of a man who was forced to take the warrior's road one night in the fall of 1987 after an explosive combination of alcohol, jealousy and firearms ended in violence, gunplay and shrieking terror.

"I was out on a routine patrol that night," the forty-seven-year-old officer recalls. "My superior officer, Captain Mike Parker, was with me in the car, and we were pretty much checking out the local highways, looking for speeders, drunk drivers, the usual stuff we do every day."

Morsette and his eighteen fellow officers, fourteen of them uniformed, four detectives, cover an area of 1.5 million acres. The winter population of the reservation is fourteen thousand. During the summer, when the tourists arrive, this number swells to almost three million, but the strength of the police force remains the same.

"It was getting late, maybe close to midnight when we got a call to attend a domestic disturbance in Browning," Morsette says. "The address given was 705 Low Rent, and we drove on down there .

"When me and the captain arrived, there were other officers already at the scene. Then a girl came rushing out of the house, screaming: 'My mother's still in there. He's got a gun, and he says he's gonna kill her.'"

"Who has a gun?" Morsette asked the hysterical teenager. "Who is threatening your mother?"

"It's her boyfriend," the girl sobbed. "He's drunk and he's acting crazy. He's got a rifle and he says he's going to shoot her. He's pointing the gun at Mom's head and he says he's gonna blow her brains out."

The teenager threw her arms around Officer Morsette's ample shoulders. "Do something," she begged. "Do something before he kills her."

Morsette gently pried the girl's arms off his shoulders and told the hysterical teenager to talk to the other officers. Then he walked across to the front of the house.

"Kenneth, be careful," Captain Parker warned. "Just check it out. I don't want to take an army in there. But if it looks bad, call out for help and we'll come running."

"The door was wide open so I went inside," Morsette recalls. "There was no one in the living room, and the house seemed pretty quiet. I walked into the kitchen, looked around and saw nothing suspicious. That's when I heard this screaming and hollering coming from down the hall."

The cautious cop pulled his .357 Smith and Wesson Model 686 and cat-footed it down the hallway.

"There was a bedroom there and the door was closed," he says. "From the other side of the door I heard this woman's voice. She was screaming and crying: 'No . . . no, Tim! Please don't kill me . . . Please don't kill me.'

"I opened the door and there was a young man standing there. He was holding a .243 bolt-action Winchester hunting rifle, pointing it at a woman who was on the floor, on her knees. The woman's hands were up in the air, and she was begging the man for mercy, begging him not to shoot her. Tears were rolling down her cheeks and she kept saying, 'Don't kill me, Tim. Oh, please don't kill me.'

"As soon as I opened the door, the man, his name was Tim Phillips, swung the Winchester around, pointing it at my head. Drunk as he was, he was very fast. His finger was on the trigger of the rifle and his eyes were looking right at me. I didn't like that look. But me, I had no time to be afraid, and I had no time to think the thing through. I did know that if I shot this man, his finger could tighten on the trigger in a reflex action as soon as my bullet hit. Then we'd both be dead. So I grabbed for the barrel of the rifle, and Phillips fell over backwards, with me on top of him. He was pretty big, maybe six foot tall and 180 pounds, and we both ended up rassling for the gun all over the bed."

During the desperate battle on the bed for possession of the Winchester, Phillips managed to squeeze off a shot. The rifle muzzle was alongside Officer Morsette's left ear when the gun discharged. The bullet missed, but the deafening *bang!* was close enough for the sound to daze him.

Eyes rolling in his head, ears ringing, the courageous cop desperately hung on to the rifle, knowing he was now fighting for his life. But within a few seconds of the shot, the bedroom door burst open and Captain Parker and another officer ran in, guns drawn.

The two cops grabbed Phillips and wrestled the rifle from him. Still dazed from the concussion of the rifle shot, the exhausted Morsette looked up from the crumpled bed and smiled. "Am I glad to see you guys."

■　　　■　　　■

On September 8, 1988, a very surprised Officer Morsette received a letter in the mail. It came from the Federal Bureau of Investigation in Butte, Montana, and was signed by Toby M. Harding, the special agent in charge of Indian Affairs.

The letter read:

Dear Mr. Morsette:

I recently learned of the important role you played in preventing a potential homicide on the Blackfeet Indian reservation. Thanks in large measure to your efforts, no one was hurt or killed, and an armed subject was subdued and arrested.

On September 11, 1987, you responded to a domestic disturbance in which Tim Phillips was pointing a loaded .223 (sic) Winchester rifle at Linda Warden, and threatening to kill her. Without delay, and at great personal risk, you entered the bedroom and wrestled with Phillips, attempting to gain control of the weapon. During the struggle, Phillips fired a single shot, which narrowly missed your head, before you were finally able to subdue Phillips.

You are to be commended for your exemplary performance in this matter. Your bravery, judgement, and decisive action represent the epitome of police professionalism. It is to your credit that Phillips was eventually convicted.

The FBI is fortunate to work with people of your
caliber . . . Congratulations on a job well done.

A few weeks later another letter came, this time from
Washington, D.C., signed by Secretary of the Interior
Donald Paul Hodel. It read:

CITATION
FOR
VALOR

For his courageous and immediate action to save a life
despite great personal risk, Kenneth D. Morsette is
granted the Valor Award of the Department of the
Interior.

"I was told I had to go to Washington, D.C., to get the
medal, and I tried everything I could to get out of it,"
Morsette says. "I'm a man who has always lived in open
places, and I don't like crowds and cities, and I hated the
thought of being the center of attraction. I told my wife,
'I'm not going, and that's that. They're not going to make
me go to Washington.'

"She said, 'It's up to you. It's your medal.'

"'Well,' I said, 'I'm not going. Maybe they can just bring
the medal here to the reservation.'

"But I eventually went. And as it turned out, I got a really
pleasant surprise. Everything was very nice and everyone
was real friendly. Even all the politicians and city folk were
friendly. There was a choir singing, and a band and flags
and a military color guard. I remember thinking, Geez, if I'd
known it was going to be this nice, I'd have brought my
wife."

Morsette says that he has prayed to God many times since

his showdown with Phillips, thanking Him that he didn't have to kill the man.

"A man like Phillips, well, he's just a human being like the rest of us," Morsette says. "He went to the bar, got drunk, and saw somebody else try to take his woman. When they got home, they got to fighting, and he wanted to take his rage out on someone. He would have killed her if I hadn't been there. Lucky for her, he was able to take his anger out on me.

"If I'd killed that man, his family would have hated mine for a hundred years. If he had killed me, my family would have hated his for a hundred years.

"Any kind of hate is destructive. It eats away at a man's soul. It is better for everyone that we both lived."

Morsette, the father of six children ranging in age from six to twenty-one, is still busy disarming drunks. He calls it a regular occurrence, a routine part of the job.

"In September of '91, I was called to a disturbance," he says. "There was this young kid and he shot a girl. He was still holding the gun when I arrived, so I told him to drop it. He refused, so I shot at him. But he was way up high on a porch and I was low down on the ground, so I missed.

"This kid, he turns and runs into the house, and I go after him. I just walked up to him and took his gun from him and pushed him outside. He wasn't a bad kid. He was just drunk.

"He told me, 'I didn't want to kill anybody. I just got to drinking and lost my mind.'

"That's what I don't understand about some of the big-city police departments. They have huge budgets and the officers get a first-class training, yet they're always shooting people down in the street.

"Out here in Montana, we disarm guys all the time. We could easily shoot them, because most times it's out in the wilderness and there's no one around to see. The only witness is God. But we don't shoot them; we take their guns away and arrest them. And later, when they sober up, they're really sorry for causing so much trouble and they're mighty grateful that nobody got hurt."

Officer Kenneth Morsette has the tough, capable face of the Plains Indian, the features rough-hewn, as though carved from a solid piece of mahogany. Yet the deep brown eyes reveal the soul of a thinker and a poet. He believes that all men were created equal in the eyes of God, and that hate is the great destroyer of the human race. He is a man who will tell you that the Indian wrote treaties in his heart, while the white man scribbled his on the surface of the water.

"In maybe twenty or twenty-five years, I believe the Indian reservations will all be gone," he says. "Drugs, alcohol, unemployment, the breakup of the family and just sheer hopelessness are all taking their toll of the Indian.

"The tribes sit on vast resources, timber, minerals, even oil. I doubt that we will be allowed to keep them. Even today, there are young white men in Congress who say, 'Why should we pay for things that were done to the Indian a hundred years ago? Those sins were committed by our fathers' fathers. Not us.'

"I believe the white man will take back the land someday. He is going to come onto the reservations with all his pride and his power and say, 'Move away, Indian. We now need this land.' And the Indian will finally be gone.

"Treaties will not protect us. A treaty is a piece of paper, and it blows away in the wind."

■   ■   ■

Captain Mike Connelly, a Blackfeet Indian, also won his Medal of Valor on the Browning, Montana, reservation. He proved his bravery, not in the lethal clamor of a raging gunfight, but by enduring a hellish ordeal of smoke, heat and fire to save the life of an elderly man.

"It was on the night of August 16, 1983, and I was a

lieutenant back then," Connelly says. "I was on a routine patrol with a fellow officer when the fire alarm came in, and I was advised by dispatch to attend the blaze.

"The fire was at a series of duplexes on the reservation which have been set aside for the old people, and when I pulled up, I saw several people standing around outside one of the buildings.

"The duplex was on fire, and there was thick smoke coming from the windows. I made some inquiries and learned that there was still an elderly resident trapped inside.

"The officer who was with me attempted to get inside, but he was driven back by the heat and smoke. I began to fear that the life of the person inside was in grave danger."

The thirty-five-year-old father of four asked one of the people standing outside for the layout of the house, which was quickly described to him. In that level, emotionless voice which all senior police officers seem to acquire, no matter their branch of law enforcement, Connelly continues:

"I memorized the layout of the house and went inside. I went through the living room, which was on fire, and made it all the way to the back bedroom where the old man slept. But the heat and smoke was too much for me, and I was forced back outside."

His clothing scorched, gasping for breath in the thin mountain air, Connelly rested, bent over, his hands on his knees. He looked up and saw that the smoke and flame from the house were getting much worse, the night sky arching red above the blaze. Once again he took a deep breath and plunged back into the inferno.

Someone yelled: "You'll get yourself killed in there!"

But Connelly didn't hear. He ran through the burning house and reached the bedroom again—only to be beaten back once again by flames, smoke and the awful heat.

A lesser man would have given up at this point. He would have said, "Hell, I can't do it. Let the firefighters handle it."

But Mike Connelly is made of sterner stuff. The valiant officer plunged into the house a third time, braving a hell of fire, smoke and searing heat.

"This time I made it to the bedroom again," he says. "The room was full of smoke and I couldn't see a thing. I started groping around, trying to feel the bed, and I kept hollering: 'Is there anybody here? Can you see me?'

"But I got no response. I walked to the window and opened it, and the smoke began to clear a bit. It was enough to let me see the bed. There was an old gentleman lying there, and he didn't seem to be conscious. I picked the old gentleman up and carried him to the window. The firefighters had arrived by this time, and I passed the old man to them. Then I climbed out of the window myself and back into the fresh air."

The elderly man was rushed to the hospital, where he was treated for burns and smoke inhalation. Mike Connelly arrived there a few minutes later and was also treated.

"Later, when I looked back on the incident, I told myself, 'Well, Mike, that was a pretty stupid thing to do, rushing into a burning building three times like that,'" Connelly says.

"But at the time I did what I believed was my duty. You do that, your duty, and you really don't have time to ponder the consequences. You just do what you have to do, nothing more, nothing less."

This strong sense of duty is remarkable in a man who was not, in any sense of the term, a born cop.

"None of my family was ever in law enforcement, so I really broke new ground there," Connelly says. "When I joined the department after I graduated from high school in 1975, I felt that being a good cop was just a job like any other. It paid money so I could pay the rent and buy groceries.

"But after I'd been serving for a while and they sent me

to the police academy, I began to realize that police work was both honorable and worthy, and that I really loved it. Nothing that's happened over the years has ever made me change my opinion."

Two long years after the embers of the fire in Browning cooled, Connelly learned, to his surprise, that he was being awarded the Medal of Valor for saving the life of a man who would certainly have died but for his unselfish heroism.

Secretary of the Interior Donald Paul Hodel signed the Citation for Valor. It reads in part:

> Michael Connelly, in recognition of his courage in the face of imminent danger and his selfless response to an emergency situation.
>
> On August 16, 1983, Lieutenant Michael Connelly, a police officer with the Bureau of Indian Affairs in Browning, Montana, responded to a fire alarm that indicated one of the duplexes in the housing complex for the tribe's elderly citizens was on fire. Officer Connelly rushed to the house and as he opened the door, thick, dense smoke came billowing out. Fearing that the elderly residents could be trapped inside, and with complete disregard for his personal safety, he entered the house, crawling along the floor in an attempt to stay beneath the thick smoke and calling out as he searched. Although there was no response to his calls, Officer Connelly persisted despite being nearly overcome by the stifling smoke which forced him back twice to get fresh air. On his third attempt, he finally reached the back bedroom . . . and there found an elderly gentleman unconscious on the bed.
>
> For his heroic act and extraordinary courage in saving a man's life, Lieutenant Michael Connelly is granted the Valor Award of the Department of the Interior.

Like Officer Kenneth Morsette, Connelly was flown to Washington, D.C., for the presentation, amid bands and glittering honor guards, and again like Morsette, he couldn't wait to flee back to his native hills, forests and mossy trout streams.

"I don't like big cities much," Connelly says. "I like to be where the elk and the deer live, and where the trout fishing is great.

"That's how I like to spend my free time. Fishing. In the cold trout streams."

■   ■   ■

Kenneth Morsette and Mike Connelly are cops very different in personality, and they are separated by a huge gulf in rank. Yet, just as their tribes were allies in the days when the Gros Ventres and Blackfeet roamed the great plains together, these men share a common bond of blood, valor and service with honor.

Captain Sam Sixkiller would have been proud of them.

SERGEANT RICHARD BECKMAN
Cloverdale, California, Police Department

■■■■■■■■■■■■■■■■■■■■■■

A tenderfoot passing through Dodge City, Kansas, in the 1870s once asked an old-timer if he ought to buy a gun to defend himself. "Do I really need one?" asked the perplexed pilgrim.

The old-timer spat a stream of tobacco juice near the pointed toes of the dude's shiny patent leather shoes and said, "Son, you mought not need one in a week. You mought not need one in a month. You mought not need one in a year. But if you do need one, you mought need it almighty sudden."

The old-timer knew that it's impossible to predict the where and when of a gunfight. He also knew that a lethal confrontation is measured in seconds, and that the decision to drop the hammer on a man is not a leisurely one.

Cops and others in law enforcement know this too, and most hope and pray that they will get through their term of service without having to pull the trigger on another human being. Happily, most succeed. Others, usually through no fault of their own, are forced by circumstances to kill a man. In these cases the cop must become judge, jury and executioner. But not for the peace officer the luxury of the long, drawn-out court battle, with learned counsel making eloquent arguments for life or for death. The cop must make his or her decision quickly, almighty sudden, especially if the life of an innocent third party is at stake.

In the case of Sergeant Richard Beckman his life-or-death decision had to be made in about one tenth of a second—during a real-life Western drama that pitted the Cloverdale, California, policeman against a crazed gunman who was jamming the muzzle of his rifle against the head of his terrified seventeen-year-old hostage.

The fifteen-year police veteran's appointment with destiny began on the afternoon of Friday the 13th in May, 1988.

"I'd come into work early that day," Beckman, forty-five recalls. "I wasn't scheduled to get there until five o'clock, but throughout my whole career I've always come to work early. I live a couple of miles outside of Cloverdale, so I drove into town in my patrol car.

"I came in the back door of the police station and was walking up toward the communications center when I heard the dispatcher send Officer Ken Robinson to a man-with-a-gun call. Being a small town, we only have one officer on dayshift, so I knew Ken would be by himself.

"I hollered out to the dispatcher, 'I'm going on that.' The dispatcher then told Ken Robinson that I was on my way. I remember I walked out of the station, got in my patrol car, and as I pulled out of the parking lot, I snapped open the strap on my holster and thumbed off the safety of my Smith and Wesson .45 semi-automatic. I don't know why I did that. I know it sounds corny, but it was almost like I had an instinctive feeling about what was going to happen."

The armed suspect, who sported wild black hair hanging in tangled locks to his shoulders, was later identified as an ex-con named Ernest J. Hansen, Jr. Hansen had pulled into a Chevron service station on Lake Street, part of highway U.S. 101, and Officer Robinson had pulled in just in front of him. Beckman, a cautious, experienced officer, drove slowly into the station and quickly assessed the situation. He eased his vehicle to a stop behind the other cars and a little to the right of them.

"The suspect was driving a black Monte Carlo, which had earlier terrorized an elderly couple who were driving down U.S. 101," Beckman says. "The couple reported that when they were a couple of miles south of Cloverdale, this guy had acted very strangely. He continually pulled up alongside their car and tried to run them off the road. He then yanked out a gun and pointed it at them. The guy finally passed them, and when the old couple finally reached town, they saw him at the Chevron station. The couple then drove the two blocks to the police station and told the dispatcher what had happened.

"The Chevron station has two gas-pump islands, and Hansen was sitting in his car at the one closest to the service bay, where the office and the cashier was. He had already paid for his gas and looked like he was getting ready to leave. I got out of my car and pulled my Smith, holding it down alongside my right leg. There were about fifty people at the station that day. This is a tourist area, and the station has a little mini-market which was real busy. There were people all over the place, and I didn't want to scare them by waving a gun around.

"When I got out of my car, I looked over at Robinson and I watched him. He was approaching the armed suspect's vehicle—and his gun was still holstered. I'm thinking to myself, 'Ken, maybe you didn't hear the same thing I heard.' Maybe now might be a good time for you to pull your piece.

"But by not drawing his gun, Officer Robinson had committed both himself and me to a certain course of action, and I realized that all I could do now was cover him. I then moved to the front of Robinson's car, where I could keep an eye on the suspect.

"Hansen never made eye contact with me. He didn't even

know I was there. His entire attention was focused on Robinson. He watched Robinson get out of his car and approach the Monte Carlo on the passenger side.

"Robinson leaned in the car window, and I heard him say something like, 'Turn the engine off.' I'm thinking, 'Well, that's okay. That's fine. Nothing wrong with that.'

"The guy in the car said something back to Robinson. Then he shoved his car into reverse and slammed into a car that was parked behind him getting gas. Robinson then ran up to Hansen's car and got in beside him. Hansen had a big knife in the front seat, which Robinson apparently didn't see, and his rifle was under his thighs.

"Robinson's weapon was still holstered. He reached out and tried to take the keys out of the ignition, using his gun hand. Well, that's what Robinson decided to do. That was his decision. But it put me in a bad tactical position. There wasn't much I could do while they were both in the front seat except holler at the guy.

"I yelled at him to cut the engine and come out of the car with his hands in the air. But he apparently didn't hear me.

"And Hansen still hadn't seen me. This guy had just been paroled after serving two years for stabbing a man to death, and one thing you learn in prison is how to survive in the street and how to take care of police officers. He had totally keyed all his attention on Robinson, probably realizing that Robinson was making some bad tactical errors and that he could take advantage of them. At this point I'm sure he didn't even know that I was there.

"So I start screaming again, 'Stop!' and 'Freeze!' and all the usual stuff, when Hansen puts his car in drive and pulls around Robinson's car. All this time Robinson is still inside Hansen's vehicle. Hansen is blocked in by another car that is stopped at the cashier's window, so he smashes right into the side of this car.

"About then, I realize that I may have to shoot this guy,

so I'm dancing around like a cat on a hot griddle trying to find a place where I can get a clear shot at him.

"When Hansen hit the other car, Robinson lurched forward, then kind of fell back so that he was lying half in, half out of Hansen's car. As soon as this happened, Hansen reached under the seat and brought his rifle up, leveling it at Robinson.

"At this point I had to make a decision. It wasn't really a decision, it was a reaction. All the decision making had already been done by Hansen. He had forced the gunfight and it had come mighty sudden.

"I fired my .45, hitting Hansen three times in the chest through the open window. We don't know for sure, but he may have at this time fired a couple of rounds at Officer Robinson. When my bullets hit, they obviously got Hansen's attention in a hurry, and he turned around and looked at me. He tried to bring his rifle to bear on me, and I fired again, hitting him in the face—but the bullet jacket fragmented on the windshield and only the lead core hit him, which didn't even faze him. Hansen was still desperately trying to get his long gun into the fight, so I shot him again."

In all, Beckman fired nine rounds at Hansen, eight of which were hits, including one that entered the man's shoulder, traveled down his arm and exited at his wrist.

In the meantime Officer Robinson, who was unhurt as he fell out of Hansen's car, ran to the back of Beckman's patrol car and fired five rounds at the fugitive, none of which took effect.

Wounded, bleeding, the gory gunman now realized he had to get out of his car, which was becoming an increasingly unhealthy environment. He rolled out of his door and disappeared from Beckman's sight.

"The slide was back on my Smith, I'd fired all nine rounds, so I moved around to the side of Hansen's car as I changed magazines," Beckman recalls. "I fully expected to see the guy lying on the ground, because I knew he'd been shot through and through. I don't consciously recall reloading my gun. I remember knowing that the gun was empty and hearing the *clink!* of the empty magazine hitting the concrete, but that's all. During the fight I didn't even hear the guns go off.

"Anyway, when I got round to the side of Hansen's car, my Smith was reloaded—and the guy was gone. He was running like a bat out of hell toward the open gate of an alleyway that leads to the back of the service station. There were scared people all over the place, standing like stone statues, frozen to the spot, and I obviously couldn't shoot, so I ran after him."

Hansen ran into the storage area behind the service station, a small lot enclosed by a ten-foot chain-link fence topped by barbed wire. Sergeant Beckman knew the only exit was back through the alleyway, so he waited at the gate, a straight-armed, two-handed grip on his .45, the gun, muzzle down, in front of his thighs.

"As I stood there, I could see into the yard, and I knew that I had him trapped," Beckman says. "I realized that if we could get some help pretty soon, we could get this situation under control. Earlier, before the shooting started, I'd heard Robinson get on his radio and ask for a sheriff's helicopter and ambulances and stuff like that. I thought those requests were a little premature since then we didn't as yet know what the situation was. But I guess Ken's mind was going in other directions and he felt we needed them.

"At this point I didn't even know where Officer Robinson was. I later learned that he'd run all the way around behind the service station, trying to cut Hansen off, so he wasn't with me in the alleyway.

"I took up my position, and then saw Hansen coming back down the alleyway. He had one of the gas station attendants with him, a seventeen-year-old kid named David

Emmel. He had the muzzle of his rifle pressed against David's head."

When the shooting started, Emmel and another young attendant had run behind the service station to get out of the way. The terrified teenager would say later that when he felt Hansen's rifle against his head he thought, "I'm going to die, and that's it."

As Hansen, a spectral figure drenched from head to toe in blood, and his frightened hostage moved toward Beckman, the gunman ordered the cop to move back.

"Move all the way back," Hansen ordered. "Give us some room or the kid dies."

"Throughout my police career, which includes time on big-city SWAT teams, I've played a mental game with myself," Beckman says. "Every time I'd go out on a call, I'd later think it through and play the 'What if . . .' game. What if that guy had been armed . . . or what if he'd resisted arrest . . . ?

"Slowly, over the years, I developed a kind of mental computer program, and as I stood there, part of that program ran the variables of this whole scenario through my brain. The computer program was now running me. There was no time to make a rational, conscious decision. The program told me, 'Here's the problem. You know what you have to do.'

"My thinking was, and is, that you must never let a hostage situation go any longer than is necessary. In other words, if you have the opportunity to stop it, you better stop it. It isn't a time for talking. It's a time for action.

"As Hansen moved toward me, he kept saying, 'Get back! Get back!' And he was pulling David with him. I said, 'Okay.' He was still trying to pull David along with him, but the kid hesitated for just a second. At that point I saw maybe five inches of daylight come between the gun muzzle and

David's head. When I saw that happen, I brought my gun up fast and shot Hansen dead-center chest."

Hansen dropped, ending the incident, which, from the first shots to the last, had taken just thirty seconds.

"When I shot Hansen, he just crumpled to the ground," Beckman recalls. "At the same time David, who's a big kid, grabbed his rifle and threw it away.

"Hansen then looked up at me from the ground and said, 'Don't do that again.' I can't remember if I replied or not.

"The next thing I remember is looking down at him. He was covered in blood and he had bullet holes all over him. I'm trained in first aid and realized I had to help this man, now that he was no longer a threat. A cop can't say, 'This guy is a no good son of a bitch,' and let him die. Hansen was a human being, and it was my duty to try to save him. But first I had to handcuff him. That's department policy. Even if a cop shoots and kills a guy, the corpse has got to be handcuffed. I know that sounds cold, but it's just something we do. Something we're trained to do. Hansen was lying faceup. I rolled him over, handcuffed him, then laid him on his back again.

"I then looked up and here's Ken Robinson standing there. He's on the radio and he says, 'Well, we got him.' I'll never forget that.

"Within a very few minutes the fire department paramedics got there and we were all working on Hansen, trying to save him. But he couldn't live. He died shortly afterwards.

"When this was all over, I never felt like a hero. I did what people expect policemen to do. It's what the public expects cops to do. Unfortunately, a lot of police officers can't do these things.

"I had to go to a psychologist after the shooting, again that's department policy, and I told him that I didn't feel bad. 'I feel good because I did my job, did what was expected of me,' I told him. He said to me, 'Well, a lot of policemen can't do these things.' That really surprised me.

"I'm glad David Emmel is alive, and I'm glad Ken Robinson is alive. It's never heroic to take a human life, but there wasn't any question in my mind what was to be done."

Gayle, Beckman's wife of ten years, heard about the shoot-out over the police radio. She never doubted her husband's skills for one minute, merely calling the station to enquire, "Do you think Richard will be late for dinner?"

The gunfight was the biggest thing that had ever happened in Cloverdale, and the Chevron station rapidly became a tourist attraction.

"A lot of the townspeople had a difficult time dealing with me afterwards," Beckman says. "They didn't know how to approach me. They didn't know how to talk to me. I kept saying, 'Hey, I'm okay.' But people expected me to be different. They expected something to be wrong with me because I'd killed a man.

"The shooting took place on Friday, and the psychologist cleared me to go back to work the following Tuesday on day shift. The first call I got that day was from the FBI. They said there was an armed, dangerous criminal in our area—and his name was Hansen. My chief and I went out and found this guy, up north of town. Fortunately, it was the wrong guy and everything was fine. But when I got back in my car, I looked down and saw that I'd unsnapped my holster and taken the safety off my gun. I can't even remember doing that."

In October 1988 Sergeant Beckman was named Police Officer of the Year by the International Association of Chiefs of Police and *Parade* magazine. He was named Police Officer of the Year by California's Sonoma County and received a special valor award from the National Rifle Association. Beckman also received a personal letter from Ronald Reagan, then President of the United States, calling him "a true American hero."

He received no award from the city of Cloverdale.

"I think the city was embarrassed by the whole thing, and didn't want the publicity," Beckman says. "After seven or eight months, long after I'd gotten the other awards, one Cloverdale resident wrote letters to the local newspaper, and she asked why I'd received nothing from the city. She said, 'This is a disgrace,' and stuff like that. I think that pissed off the city a little bit, because they eventually presented me with a little typed-up thing in a twenty-nine-cent tin frame.

"The real important awards to me were the letters I got from kids all over the country, over two hundred of them. They asked for a photograph and what it was like to be a policeman. I really got a kick out of that.

"Then David Emmel's mother came down to the station and said, 'Thank you for saving my son's life.' And that was real nice. Ken Robinson saw me in the police station after the shooting, and he said, 'You saved my life, Richard.' That was the only time he mentioned it. I said, 'I was only doing my job, Ken. Don't worry about it.'

"The police dispatcher gave me a hug when I got back. That doesn't happen in police work. Female employees don't hug the officers. But she was so pleased that we were all okay that she just ran up and hugged me. I liked that.

"I think that Ernest Hansen should never have been on the streets. He should have been in prison. He stabbed a guy to death, then tried to hide the body, and he did hardly any time in jail. Just two years. When it came down to it, it was his decision to die. It wasn't mine. He made the decision. And he died. I was just the instrument of his decision.

"This is my story. It's what happened to me. I wanted to tell it so that it wouldn't be butchered up and cut short. It needs time to tell.

"When a cop takes a human life, he's got to tell himself that he was doing his job, the job the public expects him to do. If he tells himself that, he then can get on with his own life. A cop is trained to do a certain job, and that computer program of his must run through his mind when he's under stress during a lethal confrontation. My own personal program kept changing scenarios as the action changed. Hansen in the car. Hansen's got Ken. Hansen out of the car. Hansen running. Hansen with a hostage. If you had to make an individual decision on all of these things, you'd never get the job done.

"Police officers all over the country have these inbuilt computers, thanks to their training. That's why a civilian will look at something a cop does and say, 'Gee, I couldn't do that.' But it's all a matter of training and the right mental attitude.

"A cop's got to be a survivor because the bad guys are survivors. They learn all about survival in prison and on the streets. I looked at Hansen right through the windshield of his car during the shoot-out, and our eyes met. There is no doubt in my mind that he thought he was going to survive, that he would walk away from the gunfight the winner. Even when I handcuffed him and rolled him over and he was shot through and through, he still had a look in his eyes that said, 'You son of a bitch, I'm gonna survive this.' He thought that right up to the moment he died."

David Emmel's mother, Mary says, "The fact is, the right person is dead and my son is alive. For that I will always be grateful."

IN THE LINE OF DUTY . . .

OFFICER KENNETH WREDE
West Covina, California,
Police Department

■■■■■■■■■■■■■■■■■■■■■

In August 1983, Officer Kenneth Scott Wrede died at the hands of a drug-crazed nonentity, who later bragged about how he'd blown away a cop.

Officer Wrede was writing a traffic ticket when a woman stopped and told him a man was acting suspiciously nearby. The twenty-six-year-old, who had been a cop for three years, went to investigate and found Michael Anthony Jackson staggering down the street.

Officer Wrede walked up to the man and started to talk to him, but Jackson ignored him. To get Jackson's attention, the young cop tapped the man lightly on the back of the legs with his stick. Jackson, high on PCP, flew into a rage. He ripped a support stake from a tree and attacked the officer, tearing the silver badge from his shirt.

Badly beaten, Officer Wrede retreated to his patrol car and called for help. At the same time he did his best to talk Jackson out of his killing rage.

"That was just like Kenny, always the peacemaker," says his mother, Marianne. "He tried to use restraint when he tried to apprehend Jackson, and that restraint cost him his life."

Jackson finally reached into Officer Wrede's patrol car

and ripped the shotgun from its locked mounts. This required almost superhuman strength, one of the effects the drug Angel Dust has on the human body. Jackson raised the shotgun and fired into Kenneth Wrede's face, killing the young cop instantly.

Later—it took several officers and a police dog to arrest him—Johnson bragged about how brave he was, and how he'd so easily killed a cop. But in court, like most of his kind, he changed his tune. He whined that he was so "whacked out" on PCP he couldn't remember a thing that happened that day and was therefore innocent. Fortunately, the jury saw right through his defense. Johnson was convicted of Officer Wrede's murder and sentenced to die in the gas chamber.

Prosecutor John Ouderkirk said later: "The moral to the story is that you can't get high on illegal and dangerous drugs, run around and commit violent crimes and then say, 'It wasn't my fault.'

Kenneth Wrede's parents, Kenneth and Marianne, are comforted by the fact that Jackson received a death sentence. Unlike the experiences of many survivors of murdered police officers, the couple found court officials sensitive to their concerns and supportive of their fight to bring their son's killer to justice.

But still, Kenneth's death has left a void in their lives they will never be able to fill.

"He was just such a super kid," Marianne says. "After he died, a lady sent me a letter. She said she just wanted to tell me how great Kenny had been with her little girl. Kenny had been driving by right after the child's cat had been run over and killed. Kenny stopped, got out of his car and comforted the little girl."

In fact Officer Wrede was so good with kids, he had been assigned the delicate and sensitive task of interviewing sexually abused children.

Kenneth Wrede left a wife, his parents and three sisters to grieve for him. Each has coped with his death in different ways.

His wife, Denel, went through her own personal nightmare, then remarried and had a child. She says she will never forget Kenny, but has now begun to rebuild her life in a way that is not possible for the dead officer's parents. Psychiatric counseling has helped, and so has the Wrede family's involvement in Concerns of Police Survivors (COPS). Marianne was even elected president of the California chapter.

"We're constantly writing letters and making phone calls, trying to help other survivors we hear about," she says. "We're very involved with victims' rights, and fight hard to keep California Supreme Court justices who are anti–death penalty from being confirmed.

"Before Kenny's death, we would never have dreamed we'd be involved in so many causes. My husband and I will be at a reception or a meeting and we'll turn to each other and say, 'Well, here's another situation our son has gotten us into.'

"But we know that all this is part of the healing process. And I know if Kenny were alive, he'd look at what we're doing and say, 'Way to go, Mom and Dad!' "

OFFICER CHERI DEXTER
Minneapolis, Minnesota, Police Department

■■■■■■■■■■■■■■■■■■■■■■■■■

Eight-months pregnant, Police Officer Cheri Dexter white-knuckled her Smith and Wesson .357 service revolver and confronted the crazed gunman in her precinct's icy, snow-rimmed parking lot. The young, pretty woman in the shapeless jumpsuit, who looked as if she should be chairing a PTA meeting somewhere rather than be caught up in a life-and-death confrontation with handguns, was very afraid—but not for herself. She knew with dread certainty that she was not only putting her own life on the line . . . but also that of her unborn child.

"I'm not wearing a bulletproof vest, Lord," she prayed. "You know I can't get one over my big belly. But a split second from now I could be in a world of hurt, so please, please protect my baby. Don't concern yourself about me . . . just let my baby live . . ."

Cheri saw the gunman bring up his fancy, nickel-plated, pearl-handled .38. He was looking right at her from a distance of about eight feet. The forefinger of her right hand took up the fraction of an inch of creep on the big Smith's trigger. She and the gunman were completely alone. Beyond the bright orange inset of her front sight she watched the muzzle of his .38 come up in line with what used to be her waist . . . and she knew in that instant she was fast running out of alternatives . . .

It was two days before Christmas 1989, and maybe a million miles away from the unnatural stillness of the parking lot of the police department's Third Precinct, the streets of Minneapolis were noisy and bustling, decorated for the holidays with Santas and Rudolph and huge pink-and-white candy canes. Grimly determined, bundled-up shoppers elbowed their way through the crowded department stores and headed for the harried salesclerks manning the counters of the blue light specials. Over the din, vaguely heard, a crooner told the crowds about chestnuts roasting on an open fire, though nobody did that anymore, and everybody thought Jack Frost nipping at your nose was a royal pain in the ass. But, hey, it was Christmas, and everybody wanted to get out there to do their last-minute shopping and maybe have some fun along the way.

But there was little of the Christmas spirit in the Third's parking lot that day, and less comfort and joy—just two armed people locked in the opening stages of a potentially lethal confrontation as old as time itself.

Cheri Dexter didn't even have to be there. But in the few seconds allowed to her before this showdown began, she had weighed the alternatives, and decided that to let this man go would have been to betray her own sense of duty and the honor of her department.

Strong motives for any cop these, even one big with child.

Let it be said right here that the City of Minneapolis Police Department doesn't expect very pregnant officers, with bellies too big to fit a gunbelt, to waddle into harm's way. Cheri had been assigned light duties—typing, filing, "just generally hanging out," she says. "Acting as a gofer for the detectives and the inspectors, doing anything so I wouldn't be transferred out of the precinct."

She reported for work a few minutes before four in the afternoon that December 23, and, after the usual struggle to get her stomach out from behind the steering wheel, managed to ungracefully clamber out of her car.

"I looked around and saw these guys arguing in the parking lot," she says, "and didn't think too much of it. In fact I walked right past them and went into the precinct.

"Maybe a few minutes later another cop came in, and I asked her if she'd seen the guys in the parking lot. She said, 'Oh yes, I talked to them and they're just fine. Everything is cool.'"

The woman looked at Cheri's stomach, straining the seams of her jumpsuit. "How are you feeling?" she asked.

"Big," Cheri said.

The woman laughed.

"She then went downstairs to the locker room," Cheri recalls. "The locker room is right next to the boiler room. It's like a dungeon down there, and you can't hear a thing that's happening upstairs.

"The other cop was gone maybe three minutes when I heard some sudden, loud noises. I thought, 'Oh no, that's not what I think it is . . . Those have got to be gunshots.'

"I waddled to the window and looked outside. I saw this guy chasing another guy across the parking lot, and then both of them ran out of the parking lot. The lot was shaped like a horseshoe with big, iron gates at either end, with a stretch of concrete wall. Once the guys ran out of the lot, they vanished behind the wall and I couldn't see them anymore.

"Then I saw the guy who had been doing the chasing come back into the lot and walk toward the rear door of the precinct. The cylinder of his gun was open, and he was punching out empty cartridge cases. Then he carefully reloaded the piece and slammed the cylinder closed.

"I thought to myself, 'Cheri, this isn't good. This isn't good at all.'

"I ran to my desk and got my gun. I wasn't wearing a gunbelt because I couldn't fit one on, and I was dressed in this huge, shapeless jumpsuit. You ever tried buying maternity clothes for an eight-month pregnant lady? Believe me, jumpsuits are about all you can get. Anyway, I did a kind of fast waddle toward the front of the precinct. My work station was there, and that's where my gun was. There was a cop on the desk, but I didn't stop. I yelled at him to get help and did my fast waddle back toward the rear of the building again."

Asked why she didn't just sound the alarm and let other officers catch the bad guy, Cheri looks genuinely surprised and says, "By the time I stood there and explained it all to them, he could have gotten away. I couldn't let him do that."

By any standard, this is superb mental conditioning on Officer Dexter's part and is a credit to the state-of-the-art psychological and physical training methods of the Minneapolis Police Department. Unfortunately, such training is by no means the norm throughout the country, because it takes the valuable time of experts, departmental dedication and most critical of all—money.

As it happened, Cheri Dexter was very shortly to call on every remembered word of that training, and it would stand her in good stead.

"When I got to the back door of the precinct, I saw a guy lying on the ground," Cheri says. "He was obviously suffering from multiple gunshot wounds, so I stopped, picked up a phone and called for an ambulance. Then I went outside."

The gunshot victim was Howard Bivens, unconscious and paralyzed from the impact of four .38 slugs fired by forty-five-year-old Ray Whitmore at the violent conclusion of their argument in the parking lot. A third man who fled the scene was unhurt.

"I looked around, my weapon at the ready, but couldn't see the man with the pearl-handled gun," Cheri says. "Then I glanced to my right and saw him come round the corner.

"The day was sunny and very clear, but bitterly cold. I kept thinking about not wearing a bulletproof vest. But I believe in God and I know He cares for us, so I kept praying over and over: 'God protect her . . . God protect my baby . . .'

"Well, the guy came round the corner, and he swung up his gun. He didn't bring it all the way up, just about to my waist level. We were maybe six or eight feet apart.

"I yelled something at him then. It wasn't a very nice thing to say, not your standard 'Freeze, I'm a cop' kind of thing.

"I basically told him, 'Put the gun down or I'll blow your head off,' except I put in the F-word between your and head and used some other words which weren't very ladylike."

For several long seconds which seemed to stretch into an eternity to Cheri, she and Whitmore looked at each other over the barrels of their revolvers. Whitmore must have seen the determination in the young cop's eyes, because slowly, slowly, the gunman lowered his .38, finally dropping it.

"Step away from it. Now!" Cheri ordered. "And lay on the ground."

The man did as he was told.

To Whitmore, Officer Cheri Dexter must have presented a ludicrous figure with her blond curls and her jumpsuit stretched tight across her huge stomach. But he must also have realized he was up against a trained police officer who handled her big Smith and Wesson like a professional and was quite willing to go to the gunfight if that's how the cards fell.

Thankfully it never came to that.

Within a few minutes Cheri was surrounded by fellow officers and everyone was talking at once. She was getting pats on the back and attaboys, but some of the senior officers, their hair standing on end, were convinced that the baby's arrival must surely now be imminent and wanted her to go downtown and get checked out immediately at a hospital.

"Don't wait! Don't wait!" one sergeant burbled. "The baby could come any minute. It . . . it could be born right here."

"But I didn't want to go anywhere till I showed the investigators where the guy had unloaded the shells from his gun; otherwise it would have taken them ten minutes to find them," she says. "I went outside again, showed them where the spent cartridges were, and then they hustled me away from there. Fast!

"I didn't go to the doctor or anything. I really wasn't that excited, and I knew my baby was just fine. She was born exactly four weeks after this incident and we named her Brianna."

Cheri's story got one paragraph in her local paper, and that said only that a man had been shot in the Third Precinct parking lot, and that the gunman had been taken into custody.

A nationally syndicated TV show later broadcast a dramatization of the incident, but Cheri says they "overdid the dramatics a bit."

"In the show they made it look like my husband Scott, who's also a cop, was all lovey-dovey to me when I got home," Cheri says. "But that wasn't the way it was. In fact he was real mad at me and yelled at me for going out there alone. He said I should have told the cop on the front desk to do it. But I didn't have time for that. I just did what I thought I had to do.

"My mother and sisters came over on Christmas Day, and

my sisters said I was crazy, stuff like that. But my mother didn't say much. She knows I've wanted to be a cop since I was a little girl, and that incidents like this are all part of the job of being a cop.

"The whole thing from start to finish lasted two to three minutes, so it was just one exciting incident in what was shaping up to be another routine day."

Cheri Dexter was awarded a well-deserved Medal of Valor for her great courage and determination in the face of considerable danger. She is now a deputy with the Washington County Sheriff's Department in Minnesota.

Little Brianna was her first baby. As yet she has no other children.

Ray Whitmore is currently serving time in jail for the shooting of Howard Bivens, who is paralyzed from the waist down and confined to a wheelchair.

DETECTIVE GREGORY SKINNER
St. Louis, Missouri, Police Department

■■■■■■■■■■■■■■■■■■■■

When he looks back at a twenty- or thirty-year career in law enforcement, a police officer, especially if he was a uniformed patrolman, will tell you that the job was 99.99 percent monotony, much of it a mind-numbing, grinding drudgery that slowly ate away at his soul—and .01 percent sheer terror. For today's cop, this tiny fraction of time is made up of several individual moments of sudden, lethal violence, many times close-range gunfights during which men, both the good and the bad, die in the street, staining the black asphalt red with their blood. But often out of this death and destruction come dazzling instants of creation— the fiery genesis of the police hero.

Medal of Honor winner Detective Gregory Skinner of the St. Louis, Missouri, Police Department is one such creation.

On July 24, 1986, Skinner was a thirty-eight-year-old patrolman, experienced and quietly capable, but he had never before been under fire or been forced to draw his gun in anger. All this would change that day, as the long summer afternoon gave way to evening and the suffering city began to look forward to night and some relief from the oppressive heat.

"At 7:35 that evening, two uniformed officers got a call

on their radio, directing them to 3500 Utah Street," Skinner says. "It was a code red, a holdup alarm had been set off in a neighborhood deli there and a robbery was in progress.

"When the officers arrived, they were told that the robbery was over, and that the suspect had fled from the scene on foot. The suspect was described as a white male with long blond hair, wearing a red shirt, blue jeans and white sneakers. The lady at the store said the man had been armed with a large handgun."

Seconds after the gunman ran from the store, a regular customer walked in, and the terrified owner told him, "I've just been robbed!"

"This man immediately left the food store and saw the suspect walking down the street," Skinner says. "So what he did, he got in his van and started following the guy. As he followed the suspect, the robber suddenly turned around and fired a shot in his direction. The van driver kept on following the suspect, even though the robber turned around several more times and pointed his gun at him, without firing.

"This witness then saw the suspect approach a young man who was working on his car in the driveway in front of his home. This is a residential area, mostly blue-collar families, and there were a great many people around, including a lot of children playing.

"The van driver then took an alternate route, sweeping around the area in a wide circle. When he got back to the scene, he was just in time to see the gunman taking off in the young man's car. The young man was driving and the gunman was sitting beside him.

"What we didn't know at that time was that the suspect had forced the man at gunpoint to go into his home to get the keys for his car. The young man's wife was there, and she was really terrified.

"The van driver later saw a police car, and he stopped and

gave the officers a description of the hijacked vehicle. Those officers then got on the radio and gave a description of the suspect and his vehicle and the direction they were traveling."

Officer Skinner was on routine patrol in the area of Jefferson and Arsenal streets when the call came over his radio.

"I was driving south on Jefferson," he recalls, "and was just approaching its intersection with Utah when I saw a vehicle that matched the description of the suspect's car, occupied by two white males. This car was traveling north on Jefferson.

"It was about 7:41, and the traffic was real heavy because Jefferson is a main artery that runs north and south of the city, but I managed to make a U-turn and proceeded to follow the suspect vehicle. It was the middle of summer, so the light was still good. However, I lost sight of the vehicle, but continued to drive north till I approached Gravois Street, where I observed the vehicle sitting at the red light. I pulled in behind it.

"The light turned green, and the suspect car proceeded north on Jefferson. Near the junction of Jefferson and Victor, I turned my red lights on and followed more closely. At this point I wasn't entirely sure if I even had the right vehicle. The description of the vehicle was a white Oldsmobile Cutlass with large rear wheels. But the license plate number had been given over the radio as H as in Henry, H as in Henry, A as in Adam 567. The white Oldsmobile Cutlass I was following had large rear wheels, but its license plate was HHA 653. However, I felt I had sufficient reason to believe that this vehicle was indeed the suspect car and I continued my pursuit.

"After I activated my roof lights, the suspect vehicle made a left turn onto Victor, heading west. The passenger then threw an empty beer can out of the window which bounced to the side of the road. Even though the driver must have been aware of my flashing lights in his rearview mirror, the vehicle was not taking off at a high rate of speed at this time. It should be pointed out here that I was not aware that the driver of the car had been earlier abducted at gunpoint. I thought that the Cutlass was a getaway car and that the driver was an accomplice.

"The suspect vehicle continued to drive west on Victor, still at a low rate of speed, and made a right turn on Ohio. The driver would not pull over, so I kept in close pursuit as the Cutlass drove west on Ohio and then drove right through the stop sign at the junction of Shenandoah and Ohio. I proceeded cautiously through the junction and once again resumed the pursuit. The suspect vehicle then drove through the stop sign at Ohio and Accomac and then proceeded along Ohio until it came to a junction where the street was barricaded off. I saw the brake lights of the suspect vehicle come on as it proceeded to halt. I got on the air, gave my location and informed the dispatcher that it seemed to me like the two suspects were preparing to abandon their vehicle and that I would closely pursue them."

Officer Skinner braked to a stop behind the Cutlass and opened his door. But the suspect vehicle, throwing up a shower of dirt and gravel, suddenly accelerated away from him.

"The car swerved around the barricades and proceeded to go down the north alley toward Russell Street," he says. "At that point I closed my door and continued to follow.

"The passenger in the suspect vehicle now maneuvered his body so that he was sitting on the window ledge. He then proceeded to lay himself in a prone position on top of the roof of the vehicle, his weapon pointed in my direction. At that point I had no doubt in my mind that he was going to shoot at me. I therefore lay down on the front seat, behind the dashboard, and steered the car with one hand. I was by myself and had to drive and use the radio, so I was not in a position to draw my service revolver and direct fire at the suspect.

"While they were still in the alley heading towards Russell, the driver—whom we later learned was being forced to do all this—must have figured that this was an opportune time for him to get out of this situation, since the gunman was no longer in the front seat of the car. The Cutlass was going maybe 20 mph when the driver suddenly slammed on the brakes. The unexpected halt threw the suspect gunman against the front door frame of the vehicle. Meanwhile the driver jumped from the car, ran across the alley and very quickly got behind a tree.

"The suspect, who had been thrown inside the vehicle, now jumped out and proceeded to run down the alley toward Russell.

"At that time I unclipped my Remington Model 870 12-gauge shotgun from the dash, exited my police vehicle and began to pursue the fleeing suspect on foot. The suspect ran across Russell and continued through the alley on the other side, which was the 1200 block of Alan. He turned around, saw me, stopped running and pointed his revolver in my direction. I crouched down and started to raise the shotgun. But there were several children playing in the alley, so I didn't shoot. The suspect didn't shoot either, why I don't know and I guess I never will.

"The suspect then ran north into the rear yard of a house at 2630 Alan. A few seconds later I saw several young black males come scattering out of there in all directions. They looked like they were running for their lives.

"It was at this time that Officer Willis Crook, in another one-man car, pulled into the alley."

Officer Crook ran to Skinner and asked, "Where is your suspect?"

Skinner motioned with his shotgun toward the yard of

the house at 2630 Alan. "He's back in there someplace, and he's armed with a handgun."

Skinner then told Crook to drive over to Guyer Street, so that they'd have the suspect between them and be able to cut off any possible avenue of escape.

"I watched Officer Crook drive down the alley," Skinner recalls. "Then I saw him make a right turn onto Ohio, heading toward Guyer, then he was lost from my sight.

"There were a lot of fences surrounding the backyards of the homes on Alan Street, and since the suspect had already shot at an innocent citizen, thereby proving that he was quite prepared to use his weapon, I didn't think it prudent to go blindly charging around in there. I therefore sought a vantage point where I could overlook most of the area.

"I proceeded over to a rear yard at 2626 Alan and got behind a wooden fence. This let me see down into several yards west of me. What I didn't know, and what Officer Crook had no way of knowing, was that the suspect had meantime rounded up five hostages at gunpoint, including two young girls, aged twelve and fourteen. He was now attempting to steal a vehicle to make his escape.

"As all this was happening, Officer Crook had gone to Guyer, then proceeded back onto Alan. He was now in front of the homes on Alan Street, and I was around back. Officer Crook positioned himself near a gangway at 2630 Alan, and a few minutes later saw a man answering the suspect's description walking toward him, holding a gun to another white male's head. The suspect was using this citizen as a human shield.

"The suspect and his hostage walked onto the gangway. At this point Officer Crook pointed his service revolver at the suspect and ordered, 'Drop your gun!'

"The suspect then crouched behind his human shield, but as he did that, the hostage dropped to the ground and started to crawl away. The suspect then stood up and fired a round at Officer Crook. Officer Crook, who had once been shot by a gunman during his rookie year as a police officer, returned fire, one round from his .38 Smith and Wesson Model 10 service revolver. Neither rounds were hits, and the suspect then turned and ran behind a nearby house.

"I heard the shots, then I saw the suspect run around the corner of the building, holding his revolver in his hand. He ran onto a rear porch at 2630 Alan, and grabbed the handle of the screen door, as if he was about to enter the home there. Two of the suspect's former hostages were inside, a little girl and her father, and he apparently was looking for them again."

As the terrified child and her father watched from inside the house, the suspect began to open the screen door.

"It seemed obvious to me that the suspect was trying for more hostages," Skinner says. "So I ran towards him and yelled at him to stop where he was and to drop his weapon."

The gunman turned toward Officer Skinner, quickly bringing his .38-caliber Colt Army Service revolver up to eye level. The cop saw the gun arc toward him and immediately fired his Model 870. Skinner's shotgun, loaded with number 4 buck, fired three times. The third shot went over the suspect's back as the man's lifeless body toppled off the porch onto the grass of the yard, his weapon thudding uselessly onto the wooden boards behind him.

"After I saw the suspect fall, Officer Crook and I approached him," Skinner recalls. "He was lying facedown and wasn't moving. He was clearly dead, having taken two rounds of buckshot from a range of about thirty feet.

"I later learned that the suspect's name was James Ray Shockley and that he was twenty-five years old. This kid had been sentenced in 1980 to two 10-year concurrent terms in jail for robbery first degree. He'd been released on parole in July 1986, just three weeks prior to this incident. His sister said later that Shockley had been despondent about not being able to find a job, so I guess he just went back to doing what he knew how to do best—robbing people.

"I can't really say for sure how I felt after I saw James Shockley fall. Everything happened so fast, that I only had time to react the way I'd been trained to react. When I talked it over with my wife Holly later, we both agreed that we were glad no innocent citizens or police officers had been hurt."

In 1987, as a reward for his determined and stalwart pursuit of a dangerous, armed criminal, and his restraint in the use of his weapon, Officer Gregory Skinner was named a runner-up in the 22nd annual Police Officer of the Year Award, given by *Parade* magazine and the International Association of Chiefs of Police. He also received a Meritorious Service Citation from the Saint Louis Police Department, a Medal of Honor from the Missouri Police Chiefs Association and a Medal of Valor from the Women's Crusade Against Crime.

The eighteen-year police law enforcement veteran says the incident has not changed his attitude toward police work, but adds: "It does go to show you that you can be out there riding around in a police car all your career, with nothing much happening, then suddenly one day all hell breaks loose and you're suddenly fighting for your life and making all kinds of split-second decisions. Police officers are doing this every single day.

"As for James Ray Shockley, he was given plenty of opportunity to drop his weapon and walk away from the gunfight. For reasons best known to himself, he couldn't bring himself do this. And in the end it killed him."

SPECIAL AGENT EDMUNDO MIRELES

Federal Bureau of Investigation
Miami, Florida

■■■■■■■■■■■■■■■■■■■■■■

FBI Special Agent Edmundo Mireles's seven-yard charge across a bloody killing ground into the teeth of a murderous enemy must surely earn him a place in the pages of glory wherever and whenever books are written about the valiant deeds of our nation's lawmen.

In pain, drifting in and out of consciousness as the result of a wound that had left the shattered ulna and radius bones angling through the skin and muscle of his left forearm, Mireles fired the final six shots of a merciless, four-minute gunfight that had taken the lives of four men and left five others wounded.

Mireles's appointment with destiny that day of April 11, 1986, came as the result of a hunch that Agent Gordon McNeill had about the whereabouts of two vicious bank robbers, thirty-two-year-old Michael Platt and thirty-four-year-old William R. Matix.

"I guess it was both the luckiest hunch and the unluckiest hunch I ever had," McNeill says.

The big, blond agent's hunch was that Platt and Matix might be prowling a neighborhood south of Miami, preparing to rob a bank or on the lookout for an armored truck.

His hunch paid off at 9:20 that Friday morning, when

fifty-three-year-old Agent Ben Grogan radioed that he was following a black Monte Carlo, Dade County registration NTJ 891, north on Dixie Highway, in the busy Sunniland suburb. The car had been stolen by Platt and Matix a month earlier.

In his rearview mirror Grogan could see that other FBI units were following him. Barely able to control the excitement in his voice, the graying agent yelled, "Let's do it! Let's stop them . . ."

Minutes later the first frantic civilian 911 calls began arriving at Metro Dade Police Headquarters.

"There's a gunfight going on outside my office window," reported one man, his voice cracking with fear and tension. "Handguns, shotguns and machine guns . . ."

Another caller said: "There's multiple rounds of gunfire being fired out on the street. Two cars are parked. There's people screaming. There's a lot of gunfight going on down there . . ."

Special Agent Ron Risner would say later: "There were so many thoughts going through my mind as the shooting started. The immense volume of fire, especially the *crack! crack!* of the .223, immediately brought back for me memories of Vietnam. There was the dust, the noise level, people getting shot, the inability to see the enemy at times, the overall frustration, the loss of friends.

"It was a firefight."

McNeill added: "There is nothing more terrible than a battle won except a battle lost. It was a terrible battle to win, because we lost so much."

McNeill, who commanded the FBI task force that day, describes the series of events that led up to the lethal gun battle—and the bloodiest single day in the Bureau's history.

"In the six months before the shoot-out, we linked Platt and Matix to five robberies and murders, each succeeding crime showing an escalating pattern of violence," he says.

"Robbery number one was on October 16, 1985, at 12:30 P.M. and involved a Wells Fargo armored truck parked outside a Winn Dixie supermarket at 7930 SW 104th Street. Platt and Matix, armed with a shotgun and a .45-caliber semi-automatic handgun, were wearing ski masks. They shouted, 'Freeze!' to the guard—and then for no apparent reason shot him in the leg.

"The wounded guard returned fire, and the robbers fled with no money in a large gray or green vehicle.

"Robbery number two was on November 8, 1985, at 10:30 A.M. at the Florida National Bank on South Dixie Highway in Miami. Again wearing ski masks, Platt and Matix got away with $10,000 in cash.

"Robbery number three happened just ninety minutes later, at the Professional Savings Bank on South Dixie, just eighteen blocks away. This time the robbers netted a Wells Fargo bag containing $41,000.

"Robbery number four was on January 10, 1986, at 10:30 A.M. A Brinks armored truck had just stopped at the Barnett Bank on South Dixie when Platt and Matix appeared, armed with a shotgun and an M-16 or AR-15 rifle. As one of the guards opened up the back door of the truck, either Matix or Platt walked up and shot him in the back. As the helpless guard lay on the ground, two more shots were fired into his back. The robbers then made their getaway with $54,000 in cash."

Matix and Platt fled in a stolen white Monte Carlo that had once belonged to Emilio Briel. The twenty-five-year-old disappeared after telling his family he was going target shooting with his .22 rifle in a rock quarry in the Everglades just off the Tamiami Trail. His skeleton was later found—with a single .45-caliber bullet wound in the skull.

On March 12, 1986, at 10 A.M. Jose Collazo was target shooting in that same rock quarry.

McNeill says: "Collazo saw two white males target

shooting at the opposite side of the quarry. They then got into their car and drove toward him. The driver was armed with a revolver, and the passenger, Platt, was armed with a stainless-steel Ruger Mini-14 in .223 caliber.

"The passenger demanded Colazzo's money, gun and vehicle. He then asked the frightened man, 'Are you a cop?'

"Colazzo said no. He was then ordered to the side of the lake in the middle of the quarry and shot twice with a handgun."

Colazzo, small, muscular and tough, began struggling with Platt and was shot again. The bullet entered above his left eye and exited through the side of his head. Platt and Matix then left with Colazzo's black 1979 Monte Carlo, registration number NTJ 891, and their own white Ford F-150 pickup.

Miraculously Colazzo survived his wounds. He says: "Those two guys were professionals. When Platt held the gun, his hand didn't even tremble. He shot me. He executed me. It was cold-blooded murder."

Platt and Matix's fifth and final robbery happened on March 19, 1986, at 9:25 A.M. The gunmen hit the Barnett Bank on South Dixie again and escaped with $8,000.

On April 10, 1986, McNeill put together a task force of eighteen agents in ten vehicles and prepared to play his hunch that Platt and Matix would strike again at a bank on South Dixie.

All the agents, including six-foot, 250-pound Edmundo Mireles, were given composite pictures of Platt and Matix as well as a description of the Monte Carlo and pickup truck. They were then assigned to various banks in the area, stretching from 130th Street on South Dixie to 185th Street—a five-and-a-half mile stretch of highway.

"We had a very serious responsibility," McNeill says. "We had two men out there who had shot a number of people, and there was no question in our minds that the violence was going to continue.

"We were out there on April 11, strictly on a hunch. But it was an educated hunch, based on the accumulation of evidence that we had distilled from all of the prior robberies. A pattern had definitely started to develop.

"We set up in the parking lots of the various banks on April 11, and had only been there for about fifteen to twenty minutes when we got a call from Special Agent Grogan, who was riding in a car with Special Agent Jerry Dove.

"Grogan indicated on the radio that he was currently northbound on South Dixie Highway, just north of 124th Street, in close contact with the black Monte Carlo."

Desperately, McNeill now began to rally his far-flung command, directing the unmarked vehicles to the area where Grogan was in pursuit of Platt and Matix.

"Just then Jerry Dove called and said, 'We're burned. They know we're on to them. They know we're cops,'" McNeill recalls.

"Dove said there was a lot of activity in the front seat of the Monte Carlo, which had now turned off from South Dixie, and that he and Grogan were continuing to follow close behind them.

"Soon two other FBI vehicles swung in behind Grogan and Dove, and I was also coming up South Dixie, approaching 120th Street. I thought the best thing I could do was turn eastbound on 120th Street, some three blocks from where the other cars were on 117th, and try to parallel the subject vehicle.

"As I passed the subject vehicle, Matix looked like a man on a mission, and Platt was busy slamming a magazine into his Mini-14. I put a broadcast out to the agents, telling them that I had observed the passenger loading up a long-barreled weapon. I said they are getting ready to go and a shoot-out was about to ensue right there.

"I realized we couldn't let Platt and Matix get back out onto busy South Dixie Highway. Knowing how violent these men were, and how their violence had been escalating, I knew they would spray the street and there could be a lot of civilian casualties. We had to make the quick decision to stop them right there.

"We had five FBI vehicles at the scene and another five were heading northbound, trying to reach us."

The Metro Dade police had also been alerted and were rushing to the area. Detective Sergeant Dave Rivers, who was later in charge of the city's investigation into the shoot-out, pieced together the various elements of the gunfight, just over four minutes of swirling, bloody mayhem during which 140 rounds were fired and nine men were killed or wounded. Like the Gunfight at the OK Corral a hundred years earlier, the action could have been choreographed like a lethal ballet, as men moved position, yelled to each other, fired and reloaded their weapons and dropped to the ground dead or injured.

"When the decision to make the stop was made, Agents John Hanlon and Edmundo Mireles pulled out of the line and drove past Agents Grogan and Dove," Rivers says.

"The plan was for the Hanlon and Mireles car to force the Monte Carlo off the road to the west side while Grogan and Dove drove past both cars to block any escape down 82nd Avenue.

"Agent Richard A. Manauzzi pulled in close behind the suspect vehicle. The intention was to take the attention of Platt and Matix away from Hanlon and Mireles, who were now jammed alongside the speeding Monte Carlo.

"Manauzzi, who had placed his weapon on his lap, rammed hard into the rear of the Monte Carlo. As he struck, his driver-side door flew open and his weapon hurtled into the street, which effectively left him unarmed. The impact disengaged the suspect vehicle from Hanlon and Mireles.

Both vehicles then hit the gravel at the side of the road. Mireles's car, which was in a tight right-hand turn, slammed into a concrete wall, while the suspect vehicle, which had been in a left-hand turn, skidded to the left and came out of a cloud of dust back onto 82nd Avenue."

Forty-three-year-old Manauzzi realized to his horror that the suspect car could now make a clean getaway along 82nd. He prepared to ram again. The fifteen-year FBI veteran charged, forcing the Monte Carlo off to the east side of the road, where both vehicles smashed through some trees and came to rest in a duplex parking lot. The Monte Carlo was now tightly wedged between a parked civilian car on its right and Manauzzi's car on its left.

Rivers says that Gordon McNeill now pulled over against Manauzzi's car to block a rear escape, while Agents Gilbert Orrantia, twenty-seven, and Ron Risner pulled up across the street. Grogan and Dove pulled up a few yards behind the rear of the Monte Carlo. Grogan, a twenty-five year FBI veteran, was a SWAT team leader and a man of proven courage. He was also the Bureau's best marksman on the scene that day, a devastating shot with the handgun, shotgun and rifle. He braked hard behind the suspects' car, screeching to a jolting halt. That violent stop would in a very few minutes cost him his life.

There had been no shots fired yet. But as soon as the converging FBI cars came to a final stop, all hell broke loose.

"Agent Manauzzi's first thought was to get out of his vehicle and back over the street to where he thought he had lost his weapon," Rivers says. "As he opened his door and rolled out, gunfire erupted from inside the suspects' vehicle. Manauzzi was hit by lead fragments from rounds fired by the .223 as he exited his car. He then ran across the street and started to look for his weapon, hoping to get back into the fight."

Gordon McNeill also had his problems as the ball opened. He rolled to a stop and immediately started to take hits from Platt's devastating .223.

"Because of the intense incoming fire, I was unable to reach for my shotgun, which was in the backseat," he says. "I left my vehicle and took cover behind the engine block of Manauzzi's car, returning Platt's fire with my revolver from a distance of approximately six to eight feet.

"At about this time Hanlon and Mireles, who had crashed across the street, were rolling out of their car. Ed Mireles was armed with a revolver and a 12-gauge shotgun. Hanlon had lost his primary weapon sometime during the crash sequence and was now armed with a backup, a .38 Colt Chief's Special which he had been carrying in an ankle holster.

"John Hanlon ran across 82nd Avenue to assist Grogan and Dove, and Ed Mireles ran across to assist me. As they crossed, a furious firefight was taking place."

As he ran across the hot asphalt, John Hanlon realized that Ben Grogan was in serious trouble. The Miami FBI's best fighting man and top marksman seemed bewildered and disoriented, seemingly out of the battle.

"As soon as I rolled out of the car I saw that Ben was standing all by himself," Hanlon recalls. "I realized I had to get across the street. I put myself in his position, the terror of being all alone while people were firing at you. It made me want to get to his side real bad."

McNeill, meantime, fired four .357-magnum rounds at the suspects' windshield. One of these rounds struck Matix.

"After firing the fourth shot, my gun hand, which was across the hood of Manauzzi's car, was struck by a .223 round and literally blown back to a vertical position," he says. "I saw that there was extensive damage to my hand, but surprisingly there was no pain, so I put my gun back down and fired my last two rounds."

Ed Mireles, who was rushing to McNeill's aid, was also hit by a .223 round. He would say later that his arm "felt like it had been hit by a sledgehammer," and that it seemed "to explode from the inside out." Mireles crashed heavily to the ground beside McNeill, then painfully scuttled for cover behind the vehicle.

Now McNeill also took cover behind the car as he attempted to reload his Smith and Wesson.

"To the best of my knowledge, Platt and Matix were still in the Monte Carlo," he says. "Thirteen shell casings from Platt's .223 were later recovered from inside that vehicle."

Agents Gilbert Orrantia and Ron Risner were also firing on the Monte Carlo, from across the street, consistently scoring hits on the vehicle with their 9mm handguns, from a distance of about forty-two yards.

Agent Jerry Dove, barricaded behind the open door of Grogan's car, now fired what Ed Mireles calls The Million-Dollar Shot—a clean, fatal hit on the rapidly moving target that was Michael Platt.

"Platt took a 9mm wound in his right arm and his right chest cavity which was later ballistically identified as coming from Agent Dove's weapon," Detective Sergeant Rivers says.

"One of the few times his right side was exposed to Agent Dove was when he crawled out of the window of his car to take up a position on the other side of a civilian vehicle. The Dade County medical examiner who later carried out the autopsy on Platt said this hit was a NSW, a nonsurvivable wound."

Unfortunately, the 120-grain Winchester Silvertip, which had plowed through the thick meat of Platt's arm and into his chest, failed by about two inches to reach the gunman's heart. The man was dying on his feet, but still very much in the fight. Platt also took a hit from Agent Risner and another through-and-through wound to his right forearm. After the battle, the area around the Monte Carlo was splashed with blood, as though someone had taken gore by the bucketful and thrown it around. All of that blood came from Michael Platt.

As Agent Dove fired the round that hit Platt, Agent McNeill was still trying desperately to reload his .357 Smith.

"As I ducked behind my car, I could see dirt and asphalt kicking up around me, so I knew I was still being fired on," he says. "I could not use my injured right hand, so I tried to reload with my left. At the same time I was rolling back and forth on the ground, trying to avoid being hit. I knew that if I stopped, Platt would get me.

"I was having great difficulty getting rounds into my revolver because blood and bone fragments from my injured hand kept finding their way into the cylinder.

"I was now fighting to survive. I gave up on the handgun, and for a second time tried to reach the shotgun in the rear seat of my car.

"I stood up, but before I could reach my car, I looked over in the direction where Dove, Grogan and Hanlon were firing. At the same time Platt looked directly at me from behind his car and he smiled. He almost looked like he was enjoying himself. I realized he was about to shoot at me again, and I tried to evade the incoming fire. As I turned away from him, I felt a breeze over my right shoulder, then a breeze and a nick on the side of my head. An instant later I felt a .223 round slam into the side of my neck. I went down in the middle of the street, landing on my back with my head pointing in Platt's direction. I was later told that the round had entered my neck, ricocheted off my spinal column, then traveled down deep into my chest cavity. I could still see and hear what was going on, but this wound left me paralyzed from the neck down for the next three to four hours."

As the gunfight raged and men fell dead and wounded, civilians kept wandering in and out of the fire zone, causing the FBI agents constantly to stop shooting and lift their weapons for fear of injuring an innocent passerby. Needless to say, Platt and Matix had no such inhibitions and kept blazing away.

One woman, warned that she was driving into the cross fire of a lethal gun battle, snapped, "But I'm late for my tennis lesson."

Meantime Agent John Hanlon was getting all the lessons he'd ever need in a much more deadly game. After the twenty-two-year FBI veteran crossed the street to assist Grogan, he took a position at the rear of Grogan's car and began firing at Platt and Matix.

"After he fired three rounds, I saw John Hanlon duck down and then get up again to fire his last two rounds," McNeill says. "As he attempted to reload, he later said he felt a breeze blow past his right arm. He moved a little to the left, then was struck in the right hand by a round from Platt's Mini-14. This round also caused severe damage to Hanlon's forearm and bicep.

"Unable to complete reloading because of his injury, Hanlon rolled over and said, 'I've been hit!'

"At this point I was lying paralyzed in the street. Ed Mireles was wounded, and Hanlon had just been hit and was lying on his back."

Platt now left his position and approached Grogan's car, firing from the hip as he moved. Hanlon worked his way underneath the car and watched Platt approaching, seeing only the gunman's Nike running shoes. Hanlon then heard the ill-fated Ben Grogan gasp, 'Oh my God!' and heard him go down.

"Platt then leaned over the right rear bumper and shot Hanlon in the groin," McNeill recalls. "Hanlon rolled over toward Dove. Platt stood at the right rear wheel and shot

Dove, who fell facedown beside Hanlon. Jerry Dove desperately tried to push himself up, but Hanlon saw Dove's body jerk twice as he was hit by two more rounds from Platt's Mini-14."

Agent Hanlon says: "When Jerry raised his head, his eyes were closed. Platt shot Jerry in the back of the head. Executed him. I saw the sudden bullet hole in the back of Jerry's head. I was lying on the ground, and I, honest to God, thought of my wife and my three kids. I wasn't thinking, I gotta see Paris, but I wasn't ready to die either. I thought, I hope he doesn't put the gun against me. I know I felt that Platt was going to kill me."

After shooting Dove, Platt ignored Hanlon, perhaps thinking he was already dead, and entered Grogan's car from the driver's side, as Matix approached from the passenger's side.

As he got in the car, Platt's foot was struck by a load of double-aught buckshot, fired from Ed Mireles's Winchester Model 1100 shotgun. Mireles, who was drifting in and out of consciousness, laid his mellow scattergun on the right rear bumper of McNeill's car and fired one-handed again, hitting the car just forward of the driver's door.

Mireles then rolled over into a seated position and with his one good hand racked the pump action. He again placed the shotgun on the car bumper.

"I had missed with my first shot, and didn't plan to miss again," Mireles recalls. "My head was spinning from loss of blood and I was right on the edge of unconsciousness, but I tried my best to figure out the trajectory of the buckshot, what it might do when it hit that sloping windshield. I was so busy trying to compensate for the windshield, I didn't have time to be scared."

Mireles fired—and saw Platt's head jerk to the side as he was hit by several buckshot pellets. The big agent once again rolled to a seated position and again racked the slide of his Winchester.

As he got ready to fire his fourth shot of the gunfight, Mireles could see Platt frantically trying to get the car started. Mireles fired, and saw the windshield explode. He racked in another shell and fired his fifth and final round. This time he saw Matix jerk convulsively as the balding gunman took the double-aught buckshot load full in the face. Devastating as that hit was, it was not a fatal wound, according to the later autopsy report.

A horrified civilian witness later recalled that the white-faced Platt, a walking cadaver, his pale blue track suit splashed in blood, staggered across to where Mireles lay. The agent's back was turned away from the ghostly gunman as Platt raised his right arm holding a long-barreled .357 magnum and fired three times at Mireles—missing each time from a distance of about four feet.

Platt then staggered back to his car and once again tried to get the vehicle started.

The FBI are at a loss to explain how Platt, an expert shot and cool gunhand, missed with those three rounds at what, for him, amounted to point-blank range. But miss he did, and at last the fickle gods of battle seemed to be firmly on the side of the good guys.

Mireles, grimly holding on to consciousness, was unaware that Platt had even fired at him. He struggled to his feet, drawing his .357 Smith and Wesson. Ten yards away, Platt, who apparently believed all the FBI agents were now dead, was still struggling to start Ben Grogan's car.

It was now that Mireles made his magnificent charge—and earned himself a raft of awards for valor, including Police Officer of the Year.

The big agent straight-armed his weapon, holding it right out in front of him at eye level, swayed, then lurched heavily toward the Platt and Matix car.

Somebody yelled, "Ed, get down! Get down!"

But Mireles, who had fainted a month earlier when a nurse drew blood during his annual physical, kept closing in on the fugitives' car.

"The newspapers later said I charged," he says. "But that was no charge. It was a kind of staggering, shuffling walk. I kept going in and out of consciousness, and it looked like a black tunnel stretched out between me and the car. At the end of the tunnel I could see the two bad guys, Platt trying to get the car started, Matix sitting beside him.

"I entered the tunnel, my weapon out in front of me, and staggered forward."

Mireles fired his first two rounds into Platt. He couldn't see Matix clearly so he moved closer and blasted the gunman with his next three rounds. Standing just outside the driver's window, he put his last round into Platt.

After taking multiple hits during the battle, both gunmen were now dead.

Ron Risner ran over and whispered quietly to Mireles, who still had his empty weapon pointed at Platt: "It's over, Ed. It's all over."

Mireles holstered his smoking Smith, then, as Bureau regulations demanded, snapped the holster shut.

At this point Mireles was sure his left arm would have to be amputated, and he accepted that with as much resignation as he could muster. But as he stood there, surrounded by paramedics and emergency vehicles, he saw a jet of blood from the side of his head splash onto the asphalt at his feet. That crimson jet was followed by another . . . and another . . .

"I remember thinking, 'Oh my God, I've been shot in the head,'" he recalls. "I stood there, surrounded by all those people, frantically slapping the right side of my head, trying to find the bullet hole. I must have looked like a crazy man."

But as he was loaded into an ambulance, a paramedic

assured the worried agent that he'd just been nicked by a bullet and that the wound to his head was not serious.

Mireles sighed his relief, then gratefully laid his head on the stretcher pillow, letting unconsciousness finally claim him.

In the space of four minutes, two deadly gunmen and two special agents had been killed, and five of the surviving six agents had been wounded.

"It was a devastating day for the FBI," said Joseph Corless, special agent in charge of the Miami FBI.

But in the days and weeks that followed there were lessons to be learned from the devastation and questions to be asked—and the Bureau was quick to ask them.

Among these were the following:

Accessibility of weapons: Agent Gordon McNeill was unable to reach the shotgun in the backseat of his car because of the heavy volume of fire directed at his vehicle. He was asked if such weapons should be more accessible to the law enforcement officer, and if his shotgun might have turned the tide of battle more quickly if he'd been able to reach it.

McNeill replied: "When I came to a stop, I was probably no more than ten to twelve feet from the subjects in their vehicle. A great many rounds were coming in my direction, and the glass was shattering around me. I therefore made the conscious decision not to try for the shotgun off the backseat, but just to bail out of the car. I fired my handgun at Matix, who was about six feet from me, and at Platt, who was two or three feet beyond Matix. I am assured in my own mind that if I'd been able to take five shots with the shotgun, I could have ended the incident right at the outset."

Shotguns, when they are needed, are now carried in the *front* seat of all FBI vehicles.

Weapon retention: Questions were also raised about both Agents John Hanlon and Richard Manauzzi losing their weapons, Hanlon his primary 9mm semi-automatic and Manauzzi his only revolver.

McNeill replied: "Both agents placed their weapons on their laps or between their legs because they anticipated a gunfight and wanted to save time by not having to draw. However no one anticipated the violence of the collisions in which their vehicles would be involved and that those collisions would cause the weapons to be lost."

Current Bureau training methods place great emphasis on weapon retention before, during and after a gunfight.

Weapon failure: As the full facts of the gunfight became known, it was suggested that the FBI was badly outgunned during the encounter.

Gordon McNeill replied: "I felt that we were adequately prepared, that we had the right weapons and that we had a veteran crew. But we came up against two individuals who were very highly trained and very highly experienced. Platt wasn't lucky with his weapon. Platt was very good. This man had bought 5,000 rounds of ammunition within ten days of the shootout, and was firing between 750 and 1,500 rounds a week out in the Everglades, so he knew what he was doing."

Agent Mireles also considers that he was adequately armed, although he has a deep-rooted dislike for the 9mm.

"It's all a matter of personal taste, but I believe a man should carry the biggest damn gun he can handle, at least 10mm caliber," he says. "To me, the 9mm just doesn't cut it as a serious fighting handgun."

Mireles especially condemns the 9mm Silvertip round, and believes that Agent Dove could have ended the gunfight if he'd been using better rounds when he made the "Million-Dollar Shot" that hit Platt but failed to reach the gunman's heart.

As of this writing the FBI is still trying to find a large

caliber, semi-automatic handgun to replace the 9mm, so far without much success.

Ammunition supply: Agents ran out of ammunition during the gun battle, which brought up the question: How much spare ammunition should a law enforcement officer carry?

Gordon McNeill replied that FBI agents, and anyone else in law enforcement, should carry as much spare ammunition as possible—more than they think they will ever need.

"Jerry Dove found himself in a position where he'd fired some twenty-odd rounds, knew he'd hit the guy, knew his own gun had been hit by a .223 round, and also knew that he'd no more ammunition. He carried two magazines. We later found one in the front seat of his car. The one that was in his gun was empty, and the slide was back.

"He'd fired all of his ammunition and had nothing left. He was carrying an empty gun when he was killed."

Ed Mireles says: "There was spare ammunition in a box in the glove compartment of Gil Orrantia's car, but when you're in a gunfight in the street or in an alley or a stairwell, bullets in the glove box are not going to do you any good.

"Carry as many spare rounds or magazines as you can, and keep them in your possession at all times."

Current FBI training reflects this statement.

■   ■   ■

If Edmundo Mireles was the hero among heroes of the Miami shoot-out, then slain agent Ben Grogan was surely the most tragic figure. Gordon McNeill explains:

"If there ever was an FBI agent that I've met in my twenty-one years with the Bureau who prepared all his life for the April 11, 1986, shoot-out, it was Ben Grogan.

"He was the former head of the SWAT team, and the best shot we had out there. He was also our best trained and most experienced agent.

"But, in a very tragic irony, when Ben's car came skidding into a halt prior to the shooting actually starting, after Manauzzi had already taken the suspect vehicle into the trees, Grogan stopped so abruptly that his glasses flew off his face. They were later found under the brake pedal of his car."

Ben Grogan had worn glasses all his life, and couldn't see ten feet in front of him without them. Within a few minutes of the gunfight starting, McNeill, Hanlon and Mireles were down, and Grogan—the man who had prepared his whole life for this incident—was standing with his gun in his hand asking desperately, "Where is everybody? Where is everybody?"

He may have died then, with that sudden "Oh my God!" without ever seeing the man who shot him.

Of all the hard lessons learned that day, Ed Mireles singles out one as the most important. He says: "At the time I was wounded, I felt like I'd been hit by a sledgehammer. I didn't actually realize how bad I'd been hit till I attempted to get up and looked at my arm.

"When I saw my arm, I felt quite a bit of shock because it was basically blown inside out. My hand was at a strange angle and the two long bones of my arm were sticking out through the elbow about three or four inches.

"I looked at the arm and made an instant decision that it was completely shattered and would have to be amputated. But I also decided that I was still alive and that there were two subjects out there who had the potential to kill me.

"I had to focus all my energy on the possibility of surviving and the possibility of having to defend myself.

"I knew I had to rack the slide of the shotgun with my one good arm, and recalled that Clint Eastwood movie where he had three words for his troops: Improvise, Adapt, Overcome.

"I had the will to survive. I wanted to live. So I

improvised, adapted and figured out a way to function the shotgun. At the time, with so many agents down, it also seemed to me that I was the only one in a position to do something that could be immediately effective.

"There is a poem by Dylan Thomas about dying. It goes in part, 'Do not go gentle into that goodnight. Rage, rage, against the dying of the light . . .'

"That poem had some influence on me as a young man, and I guess you could say that I was raging against the dying of the light on April 11.

"Every law enforcement officer must be mentally prepared for a violent confrontation, and if you are shot or injured, it does not necessarily mean you will die.

"I was wounded twice and survived. Gordon McNeill was also shot twice, one a K5 hit to the chest, and he is still very much alive. Matix was shot six times before he died. Platt was shot twelve times before he died. John Hanlon was wounded three or four times, and he is still alive today.

"If you are shot and wounded, it does not mean you are going to die. If you shoot and wound your subject, it does not mean that he is going to die either.

"I can say with some authority, that if you are a police officer and you are hit and you give up and lay down to die, then that is exactly what will happen. You will die. If you give up the will to live, your spirit will dissipate. It will disappear.

"If you lose the will to live and lay down to die, the subject who shot you in the first place is going to come after you. He will come around the corner or come around the car and shoot you at point-blank range. And you will die."

Mireles says it is the cop who goes down, gut shot, bleeding, hurting like hell, but who's as mean as a wounded rattler and screams his rage and defiance at the bad guys as he keeps the weapon in his fist spitting fire . . . who will live.

Sadly, in this less than perfect world, it's the nice guys who finish last in gunfights. A 1992 FBI study of fifty police killings between 1978 and 1982 showed that most of the officers killed in the line of duty were those others described as good-natured, friendly and interested in helping people—"the guy you might want as your next-door neighbor."

"We were surprised by the results of the study," says Anthony Oinizzotto, an FBI forensic psychologist who coordinated the inquiry. "We expected to find that many of the [slain] officers had abused their authority or were overly aggressive.

"What we found, however, was that they were individuals who typically were public-relations oriented, who considered themselves to have the ability to read people and who looked for the good in them."

∎   ∎   ∎

Doctors managed to save Edmundo Mireles's arm, and he is still in Miami, where he works undercover in the war against the illegal drug trade.

He is uncomfortable with the word "hero" and says that he only did his job and that any of the other agents present at the shoot-out could have done as well or better.

Mireles at first did not want to accept the Police Officer of the Year award, till one of his superiors suggested it was a prestigious honor and might be good for the Bureau.

"When I was accepting the award in Washington, D.C., the other agents were sitting there in the front row—McNeill, Hanlon, Manauzzi, Orrantia and others," he says.

"I wanted to reach out to them and say, 'You all deserve this as much as I do; please don't hold this against me.'

"But I guess they understood, because they were all happy for me and have to this day been very supportive."

Mireles, who is married to an FBI special agent, says the Bureau has been good to him over the years, but when it comes his time to leave, he will walk out of the door and not look back.

"Ben Grogan was due to retire, but chose to stay on," he says. "That won't happen to me. When it's time to go, I'll go. I'll have no regrets."

Agent Gordon McNeill is also still in Miami. He says:

"Ben Grogan had a favorite short speech which was made by Theodore Roosevelt when he was the assistant police commissioner of New York. Ben loved this speech, and he lived it during his career in the FBI, as did Agent Jerry Dove. We all lived it that day of April 11, 1986. This speech hangs in the FBI office in Miami, and I'd like to read it to you:

" 'It is not the critic who counts, not the man who points out how the strong man stumbled, or where the doers of deeds could have done them better.

" 'The credit belongs to the man who was actually in the arena, whose face is marred by the dust and sweat and blood, who strives valiantly, who errs and comes short again and again, who knows the great enthusiasms, great devotions, and spends himself in a worthy cause, who knows at the best the triumph of high achievement, and who at the worst, if he fails, at least fails while daring greatly, so that his place shall never be with those cold and timid souls who know neither victory nor defeat.' "

IN THE LINE OF DUTY . . .

DETECTIVE MICHAEL RABURN

King County, Washington, Police Department

■■■■■■■■■■■■■■■■■■■■

Budget cuts . . . lack of money . . . a "Sorry, no can do" from a tax-conscious government—what lousy, gut-wrenching reasons for a promising young police officer to lose his life.

Just hours after the stabbing death of her husband, grieving widow Linda Raburn told a reporter from the *Seattle Times* that the death of Detective Michael Raburn could have been prevented—were it not for police department budget cuts.

Linda, a radio dispatcher for the King County Police, said: "In the 1970s, I routinely entered the names of suspects into the Sea-King [Seattle-King County] crime computer. Sometimes the name would suddenly pop up with the suspect's rap sheet and the words 'HAZARD . . . HAZARD . . . HAZARD . . .' flashing at the top of the terminal screen.

"Dispatchers could then warn the cops on the street that they were dealing with a person who had a history of violent criminal behavior, including assaults on police officers."

The Sea-King system gave officers a major advantage— they were warned well in advance that they were dealing with a potentially violent suspect. But because of drastic government cutbacks in funding for law enforcement,

Sea-King was dropped from the King County crime-fighting arsenal. Detective Michael Raburn therefore had no way of knowing that the man on whom he was about to serve an eviction notice had threatened police with a rifle just twelve months before.

On March 27, 1984, as Detective Raburn tried to reason with Robert Baldwin through the man's apartment door, open only a crack, Baldwin suddenly drove the three-foot blade of a ceremonial sword through the young cop's chest and into his heart.

Detective Raburn died at the hospital an hour later.

"I keep thinking that if we'd had Sea-King that day, my husband would still be alive," Linda Raburn says. "Where do you cut a budget when a police officer's life is at stake?

"Michael had served eviction notices hundreds of times. But that simple, routine procedure would take him away from me forever and bring all our plans for the future to nothing. Our life together ended in the split second it took for Robert Baldwin's sword to find its mark in Michael's heart."

For Linda Raburn, her husband's death was very difficult to accept, because it might have been prevented had his police department received adequate financing from the government and the community.

Today, this lack of funding is still widespread, forcing many police departments to hold bake sales and flea markets to raise funds for necessary equipment, like armored vests. These life-saving vests should be standard equipment for all police officers—but many of the smaller departments still don't have them.

The concerned citizen should not underestimate the value of seemingly less vital equipment. To save gasoline costs, most of our police officers drive cruisers without air-conditioning, regardless of the climate. When the temperature soars to the high eighties and nineties, and the humidity is so thick a cop feels as if he or she is breathing steam, the last thing the cop wants to do is strap on a hot, bulky, bullet-resistant vest. The Fraternal Order of Police is still battling to get all of its officers provided with lighter vests—and air-conditioned cars.

If you are fortunate enough to visit the Vietnam Memorial in Washington, D.C., you will find inscribed on its black granite wall the names of our honored dead who fell in that war. The wall is full. No more names can or ever will be added. But a few miles away in Virginia stands the National Law Enforcement Officers Memorial, its marble walls containing the names of the 12,561 law enforcement officers who have fallen in the line of duty since 1794. Unlike the Vietnam Memorial, the two 304-foot long walls of the National Law Enforcement Officers Memorial have plenty of empty space. If the current rate of deaths among law enforcement officers, 153 a year, were to remain constant, names of future officers killed could be added until the year 2100. Let us hope and pray that no more Michael Raburns, because of a parsimonious government and an indifferent citizenry, are among them.

DETECTIVE BILL PRIDEMORE
Metropolitan Police Department, Nashville, Tennessee

■ ■

Murder Squad Detective Bill Pridemore studied the photographs of the dead woman on the bed and for the third or fourth time that day told himself that this was the kind of case that sometimes makes a man ask himself why he chose police work as a profession.

The woman's name was Catherine "Candy" Moulton. She had been blond, blue-eyed, very pretty and just twenty-two years old. Now, in death, she was no longer beautiful. The police photographer's matte eight-by-tens showed her long hair splashed with blood, her eyes tight shut, as though she had felt, but tried to avoid seeing, the full horror of her final moments on earth.

The naked, slender body was spread-eagled, the outstretched arms and legs tied to the four corners of her waterbed. She had been stabbed many times, raped mercilessly, and—this a final, contemptuous gesture from her killer—four wooden spoons from her kitchen had been thrust deep into her vagina. Her diamond wedding ring, which her husband had bought at Zale's Jewelers two years before, was gone.

"It's bad," Detective Pat Postiglione told Pridemore as he watched the younger man shake his head and then throw the photos onto his desk. "I think it's about as bad as any I've seen."

Pridemore nodded. "It's bad all right, Pat. What have we got on it?"

Now it was Postiglione's turn to shake his head. "Very little," the detective said. "We're starting from scratch on this one."

Pridemore, of the Nashville Police Department, was no stranger to violent death. He'd seen it many times. But his usual beat was the streets of the city where the drug dealers operated and often shot one another or their clients. Death was a man lying in the rain in the gutter in gold chains and diamond rings while better men took notes and measurements and wearily went through the motions of finding his killer. This was death as Bill Pridemore knew it.

Candy Moulton's death was very different. The deeply religious Seventh Day Adventist had been mixing cookie dough in her kitchen when her killer struck, and her laundry had been spinning in the dryer. She had not deserved to die like this.

Candy, who had no children, had been an administrative assistant for a real estate broker. Her supervisor, Jacqueline Kelly, told Pridemore later that Candy Moulton was "just a wonderful girl" who was allowed to take time off the job to attend church services on Fridays and Saturdays.

"I'd encouraged her to go to school and go after her real estate license," Kelly said. "She was going to take her real estate examination this Thursday. She couldn't have been prettier. She was so striking, a natural beauty. She had just beautiful long, blond hair. She was very reliable, very honest and willing to do anything to make the office run smoothly.

"I still can't get over it. I can't imagine why anyone would want to hurt her. It would be different if she was the type to drink and run around, but she wasn't.

"She was probably the kindest, gentlest young lady I've ever known."

Something possessed Bill Pridemore as he looked at the photos of Candy Moulton's bedroom that day, took hold of him and wouldn't let go. He knew as he sat back in his battered swivel chair and looked again at the mutilated, outraged body on the bed that he would never let this drop. He made a solemn vow to himself then to track down the dead girl's killer—no matter how long it took.

This is a book about courage. According to the *World Book Dictionary*, courage is "moral strength that makes a person face any danger, trouble or pain steadily and without showing fear." But courage manifests itself in many different ways. The cop who goes down with a bullet in his chest, his 9mm spitting lead as he screams his rage and defiance at the bad guys, shows one kind. This is a white-hot, blazing courage that lasts for a very few seconds and then it's gone. And when it's over, a man often pokes through the cold ashes of it in his mind and can't remember how it felt or how it happened. Then there is courage of another kind. This doesn't burn as brightly, but it burns long. This is the courage of the mountain climber and not the courage of the bullfighter, the courage of the thinker and not the fighter. This courage is quieter, less flashy perhaps, but just as real, and it too is the ultimate measure of the man.

Detective Bill Pridemore is a man of such quiet courage, in his case coupled with a bulldog tenacity and the will to see a job through to its end. In the space of just over a year, Pridemore knocked on hundreds of doors and fingerprinted more than a thousand men as he battled to solve the mystery of Candy Moulton's vicious rape-slaying.

He didn't have to do it. He had other cases to solve, and he could have left the Moulton case to fellow officers who were just as competent as himself. But what Pridemore saw that day in Candy's bedroom sickened him so much that it stuck deep in his craw, and he knew he couldn't rest until he found her killer and brought him to justice.

The case that tested the outer limits of Bill Pridemore's courage and endurance began on Father's Day, Sunday, June 18, 1989, the day Candy's body was found in the apartment she shared with her husband in Nashville's Harding Mall area, a vast, integrated, middle-class housing complex populated in about equal proportion by Caucasian, Afro-American and Hispanic residents.

Candy's husband Kenneth, a flight instructor at Smyrna Airport, returned home at 6 P.M. to Apartment 14 at the Dominion House complex. He called out to his wife as he opened the door, but she didn't answer. Still calling her name, he tried the kitchen. She wasn't there, but he saw a bowl of cookie dough lying on the counter. He smiled. Candy was always baking cookies for somebody.

"Hey, Candy, I'm home!" Kenneth Moulton called again. Then he walked into the bedroom . . .

■   ■   ■

"The Murder Squad, as opposed to the regular Homicide Department, is called only in cases where there are no witnesses and no suspects," thirty-eight-year-old Pridemore says. "The Homicide investigator is first at the scene, and he then makes the determination if this is something the Murder Squad should be called out on.

"When the Candy Moulton murder happened, I was on a golfing trip and another Murder Squad detective, Pat Postiglione, was assigned to the case. Two days later, all seven Murder Squad detectives, including myself, were assigned to the case. Then Pat's brother passed away in New York City, and he had to leave, and I was told to lead the investigation."

Pridemore retraced the steps already taken by the competent, methodical Postiglione. He learned that Candy had been working part-time while her husband was going to school at Middle State University, taking aviation. Kenneth Moulton, who is now a pilot for a major airline, had just graduated a few weeks before his wife's death.

"On the day of Candy's death, her husband had left home at 9 A.M. to drive to the airport, about twenty minutes away, where he was giving flying lessons to build up his hours in twin-engine aircraft," Pridemore says.

"Candy left about the same time to go to the grocery store. She was planning a birthday party for her little cousin and needed some ingredients for cookies.

"When she got back from the store, Candy left her groceries out while she carried some clothes down to the laundry room. As far as we know, she went down there at least twice. When she came back, she started making some cookie dough.

"While she was putting the cookies onto a baking tray, her attacker grabbed her from behind. She had a wooden spoon in her hand, and apparently her assailant grabbed the spoon as he dragged her into the bedroom. We believe Candy struggled desperately, because her earring was later found in the kitchen."

Pridemore says that once in the bedroom, the woman's assailant used a knife to cut off all of her clothes, tied her to the waterbed with electrical cord and then "raped her in every conceivable way a woman can be raped."

"Afterwards, the man got a kitchen knife and stabbed Candy nine times," Pridemore says. "Some of the wounds were superficial, just scratches, like he was slowly building up to it. The last three or four were in the chest, very deep and deadly.

"After he did this, the killer went into the kitchen and got the wooden spoons she used in her baking and pushed them into her vagina."

The manager of the apartment complex told Postiglione

that several women who lived in the apartments had been "approached" by a young black male the day before Candy's murder.

On the Monday following the murder, Pridemore had some questionnaires made up and distributed them to the residents of the two hundred–odd apartments in Candy Moulton's complex. He then followed up on each one, knocking on doors, establishing who had been around that Sunday and who hadn't.

"That's when we found five different women who had been approached one way or another by a male black on Saturday afternoon," Pridemore says. "All said the man had been wearing a purple shirt.

"His approach to these women showed an escalating pattern of violence. Early in the day he'd just said hello to a couple of women in the laundry room. But by the Saturday evening his approach was increasingly violent. He finally knocked one of the women down, and she later reported the incident as a purse-snatching attempt. But when we started to talk to her, and she recalled more of the details, she suddenly realized he wasn't trying to get her purse—he was trying to get her."

Pridemore then called the FBI's Behavioral Science Unit in Washington, D.C., and asked if they could supply a profile of the killer and suggest a direction for his investigation.

"This man is young, strong and has probably never killed before," an FBI agent told the detective. "Our reason for believing that he is a first-time murderer is that he experimented with the knife before he delivered the final fatal blows, making a few shallow cuts, testing how to go about it. And the wooden spoons were not shoved very far into the victim's vagina. This also suggests that he was experimenting, just trying some things out for the first time."

Pridemore, stocky, intelligent and good-natured, recovered some hairs from the victim's body that were not hers. These were later analyzed and confirmed to be of Negroid origin.

"There were now seven of us on the case, and we sat down with the manager of the apartment complex and she gave us a roster of everyone who lived in the building," he recalls. "The trouble was, Candy Moulton's complex was surrounded by four more apartment complexes. One complex had over three hundred apartments, one had five hundred and another had over a thousand."

In Pridemore's office that afternoon the detectives plotted their next moves. "You're calling the shots, Bill," one of the investigators said. "Where do we go from here?"

Pridemore smiled. "We start knocking on doors."

"That's nearly two thousand apartments," Postiglione said. "It's going to take time. A lot of legwork."

Pridemore nodded. "I hope this guy gives us the time. I don't want to find another Candy Moulton before we get this thing sewed up."

Postiglione rose from his chair and glanced at his watch. "Well, it's getting late—let's go knock on some doors," he said.

During the tedious days and weeks that followed, Pridemore and the other detectives knocked on hundreds of doors, asking every resident who answered if they had a young black male living with them, and if he could be interviewed.

"In the meantime, we had the five women help us put together a composite picture of this guy, and we distributed it around the apartment complexes and to the media," Pridemore says. "We wanted to find this guy in the purple T-shirt. We wanted him bad.

"Our assistant chief of police, John Ross, took a keen interest in the case and loaned us some patrol officers to help distribute the fliers. Chief Ross died recently. He was truly a wonderful man, and a first-class cop. When we started early in the morning, he'd be right with us, and he'd stay till we finished up late at night."

But as the weeks passed, the leads grew cold, and one by one detectives were pulled from the case, until Detectives Pridemore and Postiglione were handling it alone. But they were also assigned to other murders, and found themselves with less and less time to follow up leads in the Candy Moulton killing.

"If something that looked hot came up, we'd run with it," Pridemore says. "But it soon became apparent that the best lead we had, in fact the only lead we had, was a single smudged fingerprint taken from the wooden spoon. We hoped it was a fingerprint and not the victim's toeprint, since Candy was not wearing shoes when her body was found.

"We decided then that the only thing to do was to fingerprint every male black in the six apartment complexes, starting with the victim's apartment block.

"We got a roster from each of the complex managers, indicating which apartments had young male blacks living there, and started fingerprinting."

Remarkably, fingerprints were taken from more than a thousand young black males on a strictly voluntary basis, and Pridemore did not meet with a single refusal—not even from the teenager who later turned out to be the killer.

"As soon as we explained our reason for wanting the prints, everyone was happy to cooperate," Pridemore says. "It seems they wanted to catch this guy just as badly as we did. Some of the young guys later asked us for a copy of their prints. They got them framed and hung them on the wall.

"When we finally got to the complex designated as the C building, we discovered that one young black male had been living there with his sister, but he had gone back to school in Missouri. We put this guy on the back burner, deciding that we'd try to locate him after we'd fingerprinted all the other people."

In addition to having the thousand males fingerprinted, Pridemore went through the entire FBI data base, which records the fingerprints of everyone arrested for a serious crime in the United States. He matched his print against tens of thousands of others in the FBI computers—and came up empty. Another data base, exclusively of our nation's military personnel, likewise proved to be a bust.

The dogged detective also set up a special flying squad, a mobile fingerprint unit, to follow up leads called in by uniform cops and Highway Patrol officers.

"We again put out around twelve hundred questionnaires, this time with the composite picture of the suspected killer and the FBI profile," Pridemore says. "We asked anyone who might know, or have seen, this man, to fill it in and return it to us. I got just three back, and none proved to be of any value. One was from an angry wife who wanted to get rid of her husband; another was from a wife's jealous boyfriend, again naming the woman's husband. It was just a waste of time to check these out. Time we didn't have."

In late May 1990, Pridemore got back into the C building, where the laundry room was, and started his routine fingerprinting.

"We then got a call from a Nigerian family who lived in another complex, who told us that their daughter had been approached by a young black male," Pridemore recalls. "This guy had actually come to the door and wanted to come inside. He'd asked a lot of questions: 'Is your father at home?' 'Is your mother home?' Stuff like that.

"Well, the father was at home, and he came to the door and the guy took off. The father chased him, and told me later that he planned to kill him if he'd caught up with him. As it happened, he lost him around the C building.

"That happened on the Friday night, and on the Monday

morning we received a call from the manager of the C
building, who told us the guy who had lived there at the time
of Candy's death had returned home from school. This
manager was later fired by the company who owned the
building because she was taking so much time off work to
help us.

"We said, 'Great,' and put this guy down on our list,
planning to get around to fingerprinting him later.

"In the meantime we'd set up a command post in Candy's
apartment, which overlooked the swimming pool, and we
stayed there for several months. We had binoculars and a
video camera, hoping that the killer would return to the
scene of the crime. As it happened all we caught were two
guys, flashers, exposing themselves.

"On that Monday evening we finally got around to going
to the apartment where the teenager had just got back from
school and knocked on the door. A kid answered the door
and we said, 'Is your brother here?' The kid said, 'No, he
won't be back till Father's Day.' Well, that was kind of
strange since Candy had been killed on Father's Day.

"So, we said, 'Can we talk to you?' and the kid said,
'Okay.'

"As soon as we got into the apartment, the phone rang. It
was the kid's sister calling him. He told her we were there,
and put me on the phone. The sister told me to get out of the
house, that I'd no right to be there. I said, 'Fine. Can we
choose a time to schedule an interview with you and your
teenage brother?' She said, 'Yes, on Friday.' Then she hung
up the phone.

"But before we could even turn around and walk out the
door, she called again. This time she said, 'Get out of the
apartment at once, or I'll call the cops on you!' I said, 'Give
us time to get out, lady. We were just walking out the door.'
Then I said, 'We're still on for Friday with you and your
brother?' And she said, 'Yes, Friday evening at six o'clock.'

"Now, we didn't suspect this guy. As far as I was concerned, he was just another set of fingerprints. But the next day, this boy's mother calls me from Clarksdale, Mississippi, and asks me why I wanted to interview her son. I explained it to her, and she said, 'Well, I'm coming up there. I'll meet you Friday.' I said, 'That's just fine.'

"The next day she calls and says, 'Let's move it up to Thursday at eleven o'clock in the morning.'

"That Thursday I was supposed to meet my wife at two to play golf, so I thought, 'I'm in a hurry, so I'll meet this woman sharp at eleven and get the thing over with.'"

Pridemore carried the murder file with him to the meeting. He showed the woman pictures of Candy and said, "Look, this is nothing against your son, I just want to fingerprint him, same as I've done to hundreds of others."

The woman said, "Before I give you permission to do that, explain to me again, in detail, why you are taking all those fingerprints."

Patiently, Pridemore told the woman about Candy Moulton's death, and his decision to fingerprint every black male in the apartment complexes.

When he finished, the woman nodded her head. "I don't have any problem with that," she said.

"The teenage male was there, but he didn't utter a word the entire time," the detective recalls. "He just kinda sat there with his head down. Once she gave her permission, I called the ID unit and the fingerprint guy came over. I introduced him, real cordial, and the mother told her son to go over to the kitchen table and get his prints taken.

"I asked her if she'd like a copy for herself, but she said, 'No, the McDonald's in Mississippi had a deal like that, and we got his fingerprints taken there.'

"So we finished up. It was the last set of prints for the day, and I thought I'd just throw them in my car and run on out to the golf course and eat lunch with my wife. But at the last moment I decided to run them to headquarters and stick them on the ID sergeant's desk and have him check them out."

Pridemore was on his way back downstairs, almost out the door, when the sergeant called after him. "You need to get up here, Bill. Now."

"What's going on?" Pridemore asked.

"I think we got a match."

The detective bounded up the stairs two at a time and ran into the ID sergeant's office.

"The sarge pulled up the fingerprint from the spoon and then put the teenager's print up on the screen—and it was a perfect match," Pridemore says. "We had already taken steps to have Candy's body exhumed, so we could determine that the print on the spoon was not from her toe. There was no need for that now.

"The whole floor erupted into cheers. In fact we had a party for about ten minutes. Then I thought to myself, 'Hey, whoa, calm down, you'd better get out and get this guy.'

"I called the District Attorney's Office, and we went through the procedure about how to do this because the suspect was a juvenile. We had some uniformed officers go to the apartment complex and stake it out, while I went to Juvenile Detention and swore out the affidavits. I got one for first degree murder, aggravated rape, aggravated kidnapping, aggravated robbery and burglary."

While Pridemore was getting the affidavits, the suspect, sixteen-year-old Jerrald Gregory, walked out the door of his sister's apartment to go to his job as a dishwasher at Applebee's restaurant. He was stopped by the uniformed officers I had placed there, and was "real arrogant" for about five minutes. Then he clammed up and started to cry.

Just about then his mother drove up. As the woman was leaving her car, one of the uniformed officers said to Gregory, "Do you want to talk about it, son?"

The teenager nodded his head tearfully and replied, "Yeah, I'll tell you all about it. But let me talk to my mother first. I gotta talk to my mom."

"This is when we made a bad tactical error," Pridemore says. "We allowed the mother to get in the police van with her son and talk. The next thing we know, she comes out of the van and says, 'Don't talk to my son. He isn't going to give you a statement.'

"To this day, he has never uttered a word to me or to anyone else, except when he was found guilty in court.

"After Gregory was arrested, we took him to the General Hospital and obtained blood, semen, saliva and hair samples. They all came back positive. The pubic hair matched, the fingerprints matched, the DNA matched, so we felt we had a lock on the case.

"I sat with Gregory at the hospital, often for five and six hours at a time, and he never said a single word to me. Nothing. He never even raised his head or looked in my direction.

"Backing up a ways, when we got a warrant and searched Gregory's apartment, we found he had one of our questionnaires with his composite picture on it. The picture was a ringer for him, and I often wondered if he held it up to the mirror and said to himself, 'Yeah, that's me all right.'

"We also found out later that his parents, who lived in Clarksdale, Mississippi, sent all their children out in the summer to relatives throughout the country. Clarksdale is a very small town, but there are gangs there, so the parents always sent their kids out during the summer school break. They sent Jerrald to his sister in Nashville, and two weeks after the murder in 1989, he went home. In 1990, his mother had sent him to Nashville again, and he'd been here two weeks by the time we got to him.

"It's funny, you know. I was thinking in my mind: How the hell do you do this? Does he say to his parents, 'Mom,

Dad, I don't want to go back to Nashville because I raped and killed a woman there.' Or do you go back and say to yourself, Well, I'll just hope that nothing happens.

"But it's obvious with the Nigerian girl that when he got to Nashville, he was starting up again."

Gregory underwent five psychiatric evaluations as his defense lawyers tried to prevent him being tried as an adult. During this time the teenager was shown pictures of Candy's savagely stabbed and spread-eagled body, ankles and wrists tied to her bed. According to police witnesses, Gregory looked at the terrible photos with complete indifference. "He was cold," one cop said. "It was like he didn't give a damn."

"Those five evaluations were four more than the state requires," Pridemore says. "Gregory was then sent to criminal court, which means he was automatically bound over in the adult jail."

During the months that followed, Gregory's parents hired and fired lawyers in a desperate bid to keep their son out of prison. "The first lawyer they fired, and later rehired, told me his plan was to get Gregory acquitted," Pridemore recalls. "He said the parents' plan was to get their kid out on bail so he could disappear."

On November 21, 1992, after a two-day trial, Jerrald Gregory was found guilty of first degree murder and later sentenced to life imprisonment.

"He was a teenager experimenting with sex and death," Prosecutor Tom Thurman told the jury.

Defense Attorney Walter Searcy argued unsuccessfully that fingerprinting is an inexact science with "human scientists" prone to make their own interpretation and therefore make mistakes.

But Assistant District Attorney General Thurman attacked that contention. "That print alone is enough to convict Jerrald Gregory," he said. "Is there any explanation of how it got there except that he raped and murdered Candy Moulton?"

The jury agreed, deliberating for just one hour before returning the guilty verdict.

"The only time Gregory ever said a word to me was after he was found guilty," Pridemore recalls. "I went to the rear of the courthouse and was standing at a door when he was led out. I looked him in the eye and said, 'See ya.'

"He turned to me then and said, 'Fuck you, man.' I said, 'After all this time, that's all you've got to say to me?' But he didn't utter another word.

"Someday, after all his appeals are over and everything, I'd like to go to Gregory and ask him where Candy's wedding ring is. The only thing taken was her ring, and the family really wanted to have it.

"On the day of the funeral, Candy's little cousin was wearing a ring that Candy had liked. She took the ring off and put it on Candy's finger before she was buried.

"We later went to Chicago, Clarksdale, all over Alabama, looking for Candy's wedding ring, but never did find it. Her mother took it real bad. In fact she slowly started to change her appearance. She dressed like Candy, styled her hair like Candy, even adopted some of her dead daughter's speech patterns and mannerisms. As the months passed, she more and more took on an eerie resemblance to Candy. I guess that's what terrible grief can do to a person.

"According to the FBI, Gregory probably kept the dead girl's wedding ring as a keepsake. The only way he could relive his sick fantasies was through the ring. As time went by, the fantasy would start to fade away, and then he would go looking for another victim.

"That's what we think Gregory was getting ready to do when he came back to Nashville in 1990. He had already approached one woman. It was time for another fantasy, another death."

In October 1991, in Minneapolis, Detective Bill Pridemore was honored by the International Association of Chiefs of Police and *Parade* magazine when he received Honorable Mention during the Police Officer of the Year awards. *Parade* said of him: "Pridemore solved one of the most brutal rape-murders in Tennessee history . . . exhausting every known method of investigation, from fingerprint-identification techniques and genetic coding to an extensive campaign using a thousand fliers."

"I just want everyone to know that I didn't do it alone," Pridemore says. "There were seven detectives on this case, and we all worked together. Police work is teamwork. Without the team, I would have gotten nowhere."

DEPUTY ALFRED MACKRILLE
San Diego County California, Sheriff's Department

■ ■

On the afternoon of July 31, 1987, Deputy James Bennets of the San Diego County Sheriff's Department spotted a bright red Chevy Corvette driven by a twenty-six-year-old ex-con and drug dealer named Mark Phelps. Bennets, who knew there was a felony arrest warrant out for Phelps for the manufacture, consumption and sale of methamphetamines, activated the red lights on top of his patrol car and pulled in behind the speeding Corvette.

Phelps saw the deputy in his rearview mirror, the bubble-gum machines on top of the patrol car flashing, and hit the gas pedal. Like a thoroughbred out of a starting gate, the Corvette surged forward, burning up the miles as Phelps pushed the two-seater convertible toward the town of Vista, about twenty-five miles north of San Diego, near the Camp Pendleton Marine Corps base. The wild, high-speed chase that followed ended three to four minutes later, when Phelps skidded his car to a stop on Batista Avenue in Vista, and cut the engine. Bennets screeched to a stop behind the Corvette and warily prepared to get out of his green-and-white patrol car.

He never made it. That's when all hell broke loose.

Phelps stood up on the seat of the Vette and cut loose with

a fully automatic MAC-10 machine pistol. Bennets's car shuddered under the impact of more than sixty .45-caliber rounds, showering the desperate deputy with crashing shards of glass and metal as his cruiser noisily disintegrated around him. The MAC-10, which has all the grace and beauty of a two-by-four with a bent coat hanger for a stock, nevertheless is capable of firing twelve hundred rounds a minute and is designed to get the job done. Bennets, his heart sinking, knew he was badly outmatched in firepower. Nevertheless, he pulled his Smith and Wesson Model 66 .357-magnum service revolver, rolled out of the car and bravely returned fire.

As nearby residents watched, horrified, from their windows, a .45 slug slammed into Bennets's shoulder with terrifying impact, and the gallant deputy spun around and fell beside the open door of his wrecked patrol car.

"I was the second patrol car to arrive at the scene," says Deputy Alfred MacKrille. "I saw Jim Bennets lying beside his vehicle, bleeding from the shoulder, and called on my radio that we had an officer down.

"The other deputy, who had arrived a few seconds before me, ran to Jim and started to give him first aid. I pulled my gun and grabbed my Model 870 12-gauge Remington shotgun and took up a position at the rear of Jim's car. The Corvette's top was down, but I couldn't see if there was anyone in the vehicle. I knew there was a possibility that the gunman was crouched down under the dashboard."

The forty-year-old deputy raised up his head and yelled: "You in the car! Lay down your weapon and come out with your hands in the air."

There was no response.

MacKrille fired a round from his Model 66 into the vehicle. But again there was no reaction from the gunman.

"Give yourself up!" the deputy shouted a second time.

The only reply was an ominous silence from Phelps's vehicle.

In fact the gunman, after he gleefully watched Deputy Bennets drop, had already fled. A massive police cordon involving more than a hundred officers and fifty vehicles was immediately thrown around the quiet, residential area, but somehow—despite the fact that he was constantly high on drugs—the wily Phelps slipped through the net.

When Deputy MacKrille went home that night, he told his wife Donna about the gunfight and how the dangerous suspect had vanished without trace.

Later, after dinner, Donna said, "You know, Al, I've got the strangest feeling about this Phelps business."

MacKrille smiled, but over the years he had learned to respect his wife's intuition, and he was willing to listen. "What do you feel, honey?" he asked.

"I believe you are going to catch this guy. You'll get him. And you won't get hurt."

The deputy shook his head and laughed. "You're never gonna believe this, but I feel exactly the same way."

"That's eerie," Donna MacKrille said.

"Yeah, it is, isn't it? Eerie, I mean."

Call it psychic ability, sixth sense, or what you will, but two days later, on Sunday, August 2, 1987, Donna Mac-Krille's incredible premonition came to pass—though for a few terrifying, heart-stopping moments it seemed that at least one part of it would fall tragically short of reality.

"I started work at three in the afternoon that day, and drove over to the hospital to see Jim Bennets," MacKrille recalls. "While I was in the hospital, I ran into another deputy, named Tom Phelps, no relation to the suspect. While we were talking to Jim, our sergeant called and gave us the current information on the fugitive Mark Phelps, who had been just spotted driving a white Camaro. He gave us the license plate number and told us to be on the lookout for the guy."

It's worth pointing out here that neither the Corvette nor the late-model Camaro were stolen. Phelps owned both cars free and clear. Such are the glittering, if tawdry and tainted, rewards of illegal drug trade.

"I left the hospital about ten minutes later, attended a routine call, then planned to head south on Highway 78, back toward Vista, which was my patrol area for the day," MacKrille says.

"I'd just pulled onto the highway on ramp, when I looked in my rearview mirror and saw a white Camaro right behind me. I thought to myself, 'Nah, it couldn't be.' Then I thought, 'Well, it could be.'

"I took out my notepad and looked at the license plate number the sergeant had given me, and saw that it matched the one on the Camaro. The driver was wearing a hat, which he'd pulled way down over his eyes, but as he got to within fifty feet of me, I recognized him as Mark Phelps. I called in on the radio and gave my location, telling Dispatch that I was going after the suspect."

According to Sheriff's Department records, Phelps did not know that deputies had a make on his car, which is why he confidently chose to drive so close to MacKrille's marked cruiser. The glassy-eyed gunman was also high on methamphetamines, giving him an enhanced, if paranoid, sense of well-being.

"We were by now approaching the off ramp which marks the intersection of Highway 78 and Interstate 15," MacKrille says. "I knew that whichever way I went, he would go the opposite. So as we approached the ramp, I pulled off onto the divider that separates the ramps to 78 and 15, and let Phelps pass me, so that whichever way he went, I could follow him.

"Phelps passed me on the right, taking the ramp to

Interstate 15 southbound, and I followed him. He saw me in his mirror, went off the ramp and drove over the embankment, getting back on to Highway 78 westbound. I thought, 'Well, you're not getting away from me that easy. If you can do that in the Camaro, I can do it in this thing.' I gunned the motor of my cruiser and went after him.

"It was now about four-thirty in the afternoon, and there was a lot of traffic on the freeway. Phelps immediately drove onto the center median, and I followed him. We were both doing about seventy to seventy-five down the center median, but he was steadily accelerating away from me. The Camaro was just too powerful for my patrol car, and if Phelps had just kept going, he would have lost me real easy.

"We went maybe a mile, maybe a mile-and-a-quarter in the center median, then Phelps started to pull back into the traffic.

"I thought he was going to hit the off ramp on Nordahl Road, but he drove past it and pulled to a halt at the bottom of the ramp which takes traffic from Nordahl Road on to 78 westbound. Well, I figured Phelps was setting up an ambush, so I stayed in the center median and pulled just behind the Camaro, so that Phelps was looking back at me across three lanes of traffic.

"Now, I don't know how this happened, but the people in the cars—and remember this was in heavy traffic—had enough on the ball to realize that something was going on, and they all stopped. The traffic, hundreds of cars, immediately started to back up down the highway.

"Phelps then turned in the seat of his Camaro and opened up on me with that .45-caliber MAC-10."

In common with most desperadoes, especially drug dealers who are hooked on their own junk, Phelps had seldom, if ever, cleaned his MAC-10, cutting the gun's rate of fire from an excellent 1,200 rounds a minute to about 750. His ammunition was also substandard, loaded into eight 30-round magazines. But despite these drawbacks, Phelps's fully automatic machine pistol was still a deadly and formidable weapon.

"When Phelps cut loose with the MAC-10, I ducked under the dashboard of my car, expecting my windshield and side windows to explode into a thousand pieces," MacKrille says. "But Phelps, who was firing from inside his car, had to turn in his seat and shoot back towards me. The Camaro, which slopes down at the back, made this very awkward, so he was holding his gun pretty high. The MAC-10 in .45-caliber is difficult to control at any time, so Phelps's thirty rounds went high, right over my head.

"As Phelps stopped to change magazines, I grabbed my shotgun and jumped out of my car. I stood behind the door of my car and jacked in the first round, which was a slug, and fired. The slug hit the chrome window trim about three inches above Phelps's head and lodged there. My second shell was number 4 buckshot, useless at that range, but I said to myself, 'What the hell!' and fired it anyway. It didn't do any damage that I could see, but it sure felt good.

"Phelps now backed his car up a ways, so that he was almost facing me. He brought the MAC-10 to bear on me again, and I jumped back in my car, getting as much protection as I could behind the door and under the dashboard. Phelps began firing, and I waited until the shooting stopped, figuring he was changing magazines again, and jumped out of my car.

"The Camaro was moving. Phelps was driving the wrong way up the ramp which takes traffic to the highway from Nordahl Road. I raised my service revolver to eye level and fired four rounds at him. Three of the .357 bullets hit the side panels of the Camaro, and one hit the back of Phelps's headrest. None of this slowed him up any, so I quickly jumped back into my car and followed him."

Deputy MacKrille crossed the highway and followed

Phelps up the ramp. Suddenly the implacable gunman slammed the Camaro into a sideways skid and screeched to a stop, so that his car was now facing broadside to MacKrille's cruiser. Phelps immediately poked his MAC-10 through the open window and hammered off a full magazine.

"As soon as I saw Phelps's gun, I slammed on my brakes, then hit the deck under my dash till he stopped firing," MacKrille recalls. "Phelps pulled his gun back inside, changed magazines and moved again. He drove off the ramp and down a one-way street, then stopped in the parking lot of a Levitz furniture store, just off Nordahl Road.

"Phelps got out of his Camaro and leaned across the roof of the car and fired one .223 round at me from a fully automatic Ruger Mini-14. Fortunately for me, the Ruger jammed after this single round. Phelps then grabbed both his weapons and ran into the Levitz furniture store.

"As soon as Phelps ran into the store, I stopped in the parking lot. I could see that people were already scampering out of the store like ants. I got on my radio and asked for help to clear and secure the area, telling the communications center that we had a full-blown emergency on our hands.

"My partner, Deputy Tom Phelps, pulled up about thirty seconds later. Other units then began to arrive on the scene, and together we secured the area, covering the front and rear exits of the building."

After Phelps ran into the Levitz store, he threw his weapon down on a counter and, with the hallucinogenic paranoia of the methamphetamine addict, screamed: "Help me! Help me! I'm a good guy, but the cops are trying to kill me!"

The store manager, showing great presence of mind, said, "Okay, okay, I'll help you. Just give me your guns."

Phelps gave the man his guns, and the store manager said,

"Okay, come this way. There's a place to hide, but it's all the way in back of the store."

The Levitz manager took Phelps to a door, opened it and said, "Right through there."

Phelps ran through the door, which quickly closed and locked behind him—and found himself in the rear parking lot. The gullible gunman frantically looked around, and spotted a deputy a few yards away. The lawman was balefully eyeballing him over the sights of his service revolver. The crestfallen Phelps immediately threw up his hands. "Don't shoot," he said. "I surrender."

"Don't blame you," said the deputy.

MacKrille arrived a few seconds later and took Phelps into custody. They did not speak.

"I had nothing to say to him," the deputy says. "I was just glad it was all over and that I was still alive. Phelps was a methamphetamine freak, and there is no doubt that he was a dangerous individual."

The chase, from when MacKrille first spotted Phelps in his rearview mirror till the moment the man was arrested, had taken just under six minutes. The deputy had come under fire four times, successfully dodging an estimated sixty to eighty rounds.

Phelps was later found guilty of the attempted murder of Deputy Bennets and the premeditated attempted murder of Deputy MacKrille. He was also charged with numerous drug trafficking offenses and faced federal charges for the possession of illegal fully automatic weapons.

"Phelps was jailed for life plus forty years," MacKrille says. "The district attorney says the guy won't be eligible for parole till about the year 2030. By that time, I'll be long retired.

"I was very fortunate to have survived this confrontation unharmed. But thanks to the excellent training I'd received over the years, and the sixteen years' law enforcement experience I had at that time, it all came together in the end."

Deputy James Bennets made a full recovery from his shoulder wound and soon returned to duty.

In October 1988, the International Association of Chiefs of Police and *Parade* magazine gave Deputy Alfred Mac-Krille an Honorable Mention for their 23rd annual Police Officer of the Year Award.

For his steadfast bravery under fire and dedication to duty, the shy, soft-spoken deputy was also awarded the Medal of Honor. This was the first time in its 138-year history that the San Diego Sheriff's Department had ever presented such an award.

In the Line of Duty . . .

Officer John A. Utlak
Niles, Ohio, Police Department

■■■■■■■■■■■■■■■■■■■■■■■

Officer John Utlak died alone, sprawled in the blood-splashed snow beside his cruiser. His mother still wishes she could have been there . . . to gently cradle her son in her arms as he breathed his last.

There are questions about John's death that still haunt grieving Irene Sudano. "Did he call out for me?" she asks. "Did he holler, 'Mother! Father!' If he had been found sooner, could he have been saved?"

These are questions without answers, though doctors did tell Irene that once the bullets were fired at him, nothing on this earth could have saved her son's life.

Athletic, handsome, a former Youngstown State University ROTC Cadet of the Year, John Utlak fulfilled a lifelong ambition when he joined the Niles Police Department in 1977. And he was a good cop. A very good cop. A judge once told his mother: "There are a lot of good men on the Niles force, but Johnny was four cops in one."

Officer Utlak was committed to helping people, especially children, and he often went way beyond the bounds of regular police work. He once bought a winter coat for a teenage boy who only had a windbreaker to wear on a bitterly cold day. He bought a football helmet for a kid who

couldn't afford one, and he freely gave of his own time at
Big Wheel City, a Niles safety program for youngsters.

But in the end he gave much more for his community. He
gave his own life.

On December 8, 1982, Officer Utlak was working undercover on a drugs assignment. Two of his teenage informants, Randy Fellows and Fred Joseph, Jr., called the young
cop and told him to meet them that night. "Bring money,"
they said. "There's a deal going down, and we need the
bread to make the drugs buy."

At 8 P.M. Officer Utlak drove to a deserted area near the
Gibralter Steel Company. It was freezing cold, the untrod-
den snow lying thick on the ground. The cop slowed to a
halt when he saw Fellows and Joseph in his headlights.
Joseph waved, smiling, then walked to the car. He opened
the door. There was a gun in his hand. He shot twice.

Officer Utlak's body jerked under the impact of the slugs,
then he pitched forward onto the snow. The two teens
robbed the young cop of the two hundred dollars he had
brought at their request, his wallet, handcuffs, service
revolver, shotgun and wristwatch. They even tried to pull
off the gold chain from around his neck.

John Utlak's lifeless body wasn't found until the next
morning.

The dead officer's parents and his younger sister Joanne
tried to cope with the tragedy as best they could. At one
point during those first terrible days, Irene recalls seeing her
parish priest walk through her door. She pointed at him with
a trembling finger. "Don't you *dare* tell me that this is the
will of God!"

The priest shook his head. "I'm not here to tell you that.
This is an evil world, and this is not of God's doing."

"Murder brings its own rage," Irene says. "If our son had
been ill, we could have nursed him and we could have given
him our love. This way, there was nothing we could do."

During the long, painful murder trial that followed, a witness testified that one of John Utlak's killers had said that he'd like to kill *all* policemen.

The dead officer's parents say they couldn't understand that awful rage and hate. In fact such twisted emotions go beyond the understanding of any rational human being.

Since John's death, Irene and her husband Joe have carried on with their son's tradition of caring. The Niles Police Department established the John A. Utlak Memorial Fund, which supports the Special Olympics and other programs for children. Joe Sudano and other family members formed a bowling team that raises money for John's fund.

Irene also reaches out a caring hand to others who have lost a loved one through a line-of-duty death.

"They'll tell me, 'You helped me so much,'" Irene says. "But they helped me too. I was doing it for my son. And all the other slain officers."

Irene also testified before Congress on the need to increase death benefits for police survivors. Her efforts, along with those of other survivors, resulted in those benefits being doubled.

Shortly after she returned from Washington, an enormous arrangement of wildflowers was delivered to her door. The card read: "Something to show our thanks, appreciation, and love for all you have done for us. The guys at the station, Niles Police Department."

Today Irene Sudano treasures that card, as she treasures the Law Enforcement Officers Memorial. "After the death, the shock and the grief, the most important thing is to never let these young men and women be forgotten," she says. "This is the main thing—to respect them for the supreme sacrifice they made."

STAN GUFFEY
Texas Rangers

■■■■■■■■■■■■■■■■■■■■

Big Stan Guffey was a Texas Ranger.

He needs no other epitaph.

Yet let us pause here and honor a man who was the elite among the elite, the bravest of the brave. A man with bark on him, who willingly laid down his life to save the life of a two-year-old child. A man who carefully weighed the odds and decided he'd rather die than compromise his own noble principles or tarnish the 150-year tradition of the gallant men who carry the six-gun and wear the silver star.

Texas Ranger Guffey was a member of the oldest law enforcement agency in North America with a statewide jurisdiction. The late Colonel Homer Garrison, long-time director of the Texas Department of Public Safety, once described the officers who wear the Ranger's silver star as "men who could not be stampeded."

And even as he was cut down in a lethal blaze of gunfire, Stan Guffey indeed proved that he was not a man who could be stampeded.

Guffey was part of a proud heritage that goes all the way back to the earliest days of Anglo settlement in Texas. The Rangers have often been compared, favorably, to four other world-famous law enforcement agencies: the FBI, Scotland Yard, Interpol and the Royal Canadian Mounted Police.

As former ranger Captain Bob Crowder once put it: "A Ranger is an officer who is able to handle any given situation without definite instructions from his commanding officer or higher authority. This ability must be proven before a man becomes a Ranger."

That definition of the soul of the Ranger is just as true today as it was more than a hundred years ago, when Rangers preserved law and order in mining towns, tracked down train robbers and, in the words of the Texas legislature in 1901, "protected the frontier against marauding or thieving parties, and suppressed lawlessness and crime throughout the state."

In those days, all a man needed to become a Ranger was sand, honesty, integrity, a ten-dollar horse, a Colt's revolver and a Winchester rifle.

Rangers of Stan Guffey's generation needed all this and much more.

Texas Rangers are now selected from the ranks of the Department of Public Safety. Always few in number, there are currently less than a hundred of them, but no recruiting has ever been necessary. Scores of well-qualified men will apply for a single vacancy, and even those who return to their police departments disappointed still think themselves lucky to have been even considered.

To become a Ranger, Guffey had to prove that he had at least eight years of commissioned law enforcement experience, including two years with the DPS, and had at least sixty hours of college tuition.

There are no green boys in the Rangers, nor have there ever been. At the time of Guffey's death in 1987, the average Texas Ranger was forty-five years old.

One Ranger historian wrote: "The Rangers are what they are because their enemies have been what they were. The Rangers had to be superior to survive. Their enemies were pretty good . . . the Rangers had to be better."

That's the way it was and still is—as Stan Guffey proved so well on the chilly evening of January 22, 1987, in Horseshoe Bay near Marble Falls in Llano County, deep in the fertile farming and ranching country of the Texas heartland.

Between 1 and 4 A.M. that morning, a paroled, twenty-three-year-old ex-con named Brent Albert Beeler silently broke into a rented house on Lighthouse Drive, where the wealthy subdivision juts into Lake LBJ, and took pretty, blond little Kara Leigh Whitehead from her bed. The child's parents, Leigh and Bill Whitehead and their four-year-old son, Cody, slumbered on, unaware of the deadly drama being played out under their roof.

At some point after the kidnapping, Beeler swiftly and ruthlessly murdered Kara Leigh's nanny, Denise Johnson, and left her lifeless body in the boathouse where it would not be found until hours after the final violent act of the tragedy was over. He then took the child to a vacant house on Lighthouse Drive, close to the Whitehead home—and made a phone call.

Beeler, confident and businesslike, told a deeply shaken Bill Whitehead that he had killed Kara Leigh's nanny and that he now had his daughter. "If you ever want to see the child alive again, you'd better come up with a $30,000 ransom and a car pronto," the kidnapper warned.

Whitehead felt a sudden chill of fear along his spine. "I'll do anything you say," he gasped. "Just . . . please don't hurt my child."

"Get the money and the car," Beeler snarled. "Or the girl dies. I'll be in touch with you again later."

There was a click and the line went dead.

The Whiteheads were terrified. They had heard Beeler say he had killed once. There was little doubt in their minds that he would kill again. They knew little Kara Leigh's life was in great danger.

Bill Whitehead called the police, and the case was then referred to F Troop, Texas Rangers, stationed in nearby Waco. Guffey and thirty-nine-year-old Ranger John Aycock immediately volunteered to rescue the child. The two had been close friends since their days in the Highway Patrol almost twenty years before.

Colonel Jim Adams, director of the Texas Department of Public Safety says: "It was decided that no way could we risk letting the kidnapper leave with that little girl. If he had indeed murdered the family maid, he had nothing to lose by killing the girl and everything to gain. She was the only remaining witness.

"The only viable course of action was to leave the car as the kidnapper demanded, but also leave the Rangers hidden in the backseat."

Ranger Aycock says: "We both knew we had a chance of dying. We weren't sure how it would come out in the end."

At this stage in their careers, both Rangers were big, powerfully built men, though Aycock, with his sensitive, intelligent face, looked more like a Midwest college professor than a law enforcement officer. Guffey, who had once spent a few years punching cows along the Canadian, had a determined tilt to his cleft chin, and the kind of sturdy, resolute good looks you expect to see on a Sunday afternoon behind the face mask of a veteran NFL linebacker.

The plan was that Bill Whitehead would drive the car with the ransom money to the house where Beeler was holed up, leave it and allow the kidnapper to leave unmolested. However, Whitehead's car was a Porsche, and the two big Rangers could not fit in the tiny backseat. At around 9 P.M., Guffey and Aycock therefore found themselves in the backseat of a black Lincoln Continental, covered by a blanket.

"Comfortable?" Aycock whispered.

Guffey could hear the smile in his partner's voice. "I've been in more uncomfortable places," he said.

"Me too," said Aycock.

When Beeler saw the unfamiliar car, an alarm bell went off in his head. He immediately called the Whitehead home. "Why didn't you bring the sports car, the Porsche?" he asked Bill Whitehead.

Whitehead thought fast. His voice betrayed nothing as he replied, "I had an accident while I was on the way to the bank to get the ransom money. I wasn't hurt, but the Porsche is a real mess."

Still suspicious, Beeler said, "Where did that big Lincoln come from?"

"I needed a rental car. It was the only one I could get at such short notice."

Beeler seemed to accept Whitehead's explanation. A few minutes later he stepped out of the front door of the vacant house on Lighthouse Drive and walked out to the car. He roughly shoved Kara Leigh into the front, then took the briefcase with the ransom money and threw it into the backseat. The kidnapper may have decided he'd better count the cash, because he reached back to get the briefcase again—and saw Stan Guffey.

"Ranger Guffey had Beeler in his revolver sights at this point," Colonel Adams says. "There's no question about that. But Guffey had no way of knowing that the kidnapper was unquestionably a murderer. He could have been just a young kid, twenty-one or twenty-two years old, who was nervous, excited and in over his head. Guffey had to give Beeler the chance to surrender. It is the Ranger way.

"Ranger Guffey chose to identify himself as a Texas Ranger. By attempting to effect the apprehension without bloodshed, he gave his own life."

When Beeler saw Guffey rise up from the backseat and start to speak, he immediately shot the big lawman once in the head. Guffey died instantly. Aycock, shocked, outraged, reached into the front seat and with his strong left arm yanked Kara Leigh into the seat beside him. Shielding the terrified two-year-old with his own body, Aycock leveled his revolver at Beeler and cut loose, pumping six shots into the callous kidnapper. Beeler was already dead by the time his head thumped onto the floor of the car.

Across the street, Leigh Whitehead waited in a stairwell, hearing, but unable to see, what was happening a few feet from her front door. When the shooting stopped, she ran outside to her child.

"Kara Leigh was only a little kid, but she was patting me, telling me everything was going to be fine," Leigh recalls. "She kept saying, 'It's OK, Mommy, Jesus was with me,' and 'Jesus brought me back to you.'"

A few minutes later Denise Johnson's body was found in the boathouse.

Ranger Aycock, who was later to receive a Medal of Valor for his courage, says: "I don't think we could have done anything differently. I don't know if you want to call what happened fate or God's will.

"Beeler called it. We didn't call it. When a man draws a gun and shoots at you, he calls the play."

Colonel Adams says: "Had Ranger Guffey, when he had the opportunity, shot and killed Beeler before giving him an opportunity to surrender, the Rangers would have been crucified for having executed someone without benefit of trial.

"One thing is certain, though. But for Ranger Guffey's actions, Kara Leigh would have been killed. That is some consolation."

In the months and years that followed, Ranger Aycock refused all offers of counseling. His way of coping with the death of his friend was through his job.

"The best thing for something like that is to bury yourself

in work and get after it," he says. "You can never put it aside. It's always with you. But you can't let it eat you up. Like any other tragedy, you have to go on."

The entire state of Texas was shocked and saddened by Guffey's death, during what Colonel Adams hailed as "a display of raw courage and heroism at its best."

Perhaps David S. Clark, the vice-president of Sec/Cess Broadcasting, put into words what everyone felt, when he made this television broadcast on the evening of January 28, 1987, the day after Stan Guffey had been laid to rest:

"I've had trouble sleeping nights since Stan Guffey was killed. Thoughts of his family and grieving friends have woken me frequently. I didn't know Stan well. But in recounting the seconds that led up to his death, I think I have learned a great deal more about him. Such as his *loyalty*. Did you know that he volunteered for this assignment that put him within arm's length of the killer-kidnapper? He didn't have to do it. But he did. As colleagues told me, it was Stan's way to become involved. Stan Guffey was a professional. He went by the book. In fact, it may have been his strict attention to proper police procedure that cost him his life.

"We're told that Stan could have taken out the kidnapper easily without revealing his position. But he didn't know the suspect had already killed one person. And, in a move designed to give every suspect the benefit of the doubt, Stan emerged from a place of safety to identify himself and give the assailant a chance to give up without violence. Think of the *courage* that takes.

"Clearly, Stan Guffey was a courageous man. But he was also *unselfish*. He risked his life for a child he did not know so that she could be spared almost certain death from a killer he would never understand.

"In the past few days I've come to appreciate lawmen like Stan Guffey. I'll continue to have a few more restless nights, to be sure. But if I lose more sleep, it will be due to recurring thoughts of how thankful I am for those who will lay down their lives for a friend.

"In the case of Stan Guffey, it was for a friend he never got the chance to know."

More than 750 mourners, half of them in uniform, crowded into the Church of Christ in Guffey's hometown of Brady, Texas, for the slain Ranger's funeral service. Police officers from as far away as the Dallas–Fort Worth area and Corpus Christi attended, some with black armbands, others with black mourning tape across their bright silver badges. And there were Rangers there too, tall, mature, wide-shouldered men, still bewildered by what had happened, some telling one another how fine and noble a man Stan Guffey had been, others silent, each mourning in his or her own way a deep and painful loss that cut clean to the heart.

The funeral procession of more than 150 vehicles, many of them bearing the door insignia of dozens of law enforcement agencies, wound its way slowly to Resthaven Cemetery.

An honor guard of seven DPS troopers fired a salute; a bugler played Taps. Stan Guffey's thirty-two-year-old widow, Josie, and her four young children were handed a folded Texas flag, the dead Ranger's hat and the DPS Memorial Cross, awarded to those killed in the line of duty. All had been atop the casket.

Pretty, dark-haired Josie Guffey says: "I still expect Stan to come home to get his dinner. I remember I would say, 'When will you be home?' He would say, 'When you see me walking through the door.' "

Josie, who often wears a gold pendant in the shape of a Ranger's badge, stills blows kisses to the photograph of the husband she once lovingly called "The Man."

"It's weird," she says, "but it still seems so very unreal to me. I keep having this feeling that he'll be back, that one day he'll walk through the door and say, 'Hi, honey, what's for dinner?'"

The Whitehead family, including Kara Leigh, have all undergone extensive therapy. They now raise cattle at a location in Texas they prefer not to disclose.

After Stan Guffey's death, his friend and colleague, Department of Public Safety Investigator Doug Brooks, wrote and sung "The Ballad of Stan Guffey, Texas Ranger." It reads in part:

> Stan was a Texas Ranger,
> Ah, but he was so much more.
> He hated that old gun he carried,
> but he loved the badge he wore.
> And I think he always knew that
> someday he'd pay the price.
> And when he looked into Kara's eyes,
> he didn't have to think twice.

Today, in Texas, when men with bark on them gather to talk of noble deeds and valiant lawmen, there is one thing on which they all agree . . .

Big Stan Guffey was a Texas Ranger.

INVESTIGATOR GERARD ROBBINS
Passaic County, New Jersey, Prosecutor's Office

■■■■■■■■■■■■■■■■■■■■■■

Now and again in the course of law enforcement history, fate gives a lawman the chance to stand alone and discover what he is, what the years have made him become. And when such a man stays silent for a moment and searches deep into his soul and finds there compassion and understanding, so that he takes the blue iron from its holster and steps, all unarmed, into harm's way, then surely such a man has courage beyond the norm of humanity, valor we lesser men can only marvel at. And respect.

One such lawman is Investigator Gerard E. Robbins.

Robbins is a tall, handsome man, well built, with a love for dancing and karate. He's a keen computer hacker, sometime police instructor and all round regular guy. He's also black.

We make special mention of Robbins's race because he says it's important that other African-Americans, and especially the children, have role models, men and women they can look up to and admire. One of his reasons for being in law enforcement, in the first place was, and still is, the hope that a kid somewhere will say, "There's a person of my own race doing good things, worthwhile things. I want to be like that and do things like that. I want to be just like him."

Gerard Robbins is a cop who believes that even one man

can make a difference, and he's proven himself to be right. But he is more than a role model for black kids. He's a role model for kids everywhere, black, white, red or yellow. And he's a role model too for the rest of us, for every mother's son who stands on his hind legs and calls himself a man, cop or civilian.

All in all, he's a mucho hombre we'd all be proud to ride the trail with.

Robbins's appointment with destiny began around 10 A.M. on March 19, 1990, in the office of the Passaic County Prosecutor's office in Passaic, New Jersey, and the events of the next few hours would elevate the soft-spoken, thirty-five-year-old lawman to the status of hero and earn him his page in the hallowed books of police valor, wherever such are written.

"The incident began when an emergency call came in to the police," Robbins recalls. "It was logged as a domestic violence incident. Then it was later upgraded to a hostage situation. I asked around the prosecutor's office, and was told that some guy was holding a woman at gunpoint down at the Private Industry Council Training School on First Street.

"It seemed to me that this was a police matter and no concern of the prosecutor's office, so I went back to work and promptly forgot all about it."

Indeed, the police were already at the scene in force and had also called in the Passaic County Sheriff's five-man hostage team, then a special heavy-weapons team that included sharpshooters with high-powered, scoped rifles. As the clock ticked slowly toward 11 A.M., at least fifty grim-faced law enforcement officers lined the halls of the PIC's Training Assessment Center, and the stage seemed set for a confrontation that would inevitably end in sudden, shocking violence and death.

The story behind the hostage taking was as old as time itself . . . the tragic result of a good love gone bad.

Disturbed Charles E. Lee, thirty-six, had followed his longtime girlfriend, and the mother of his eighteen-month-old child, Carmen Rojas, to the center and had begged the pretty twenty-four-year-old to come back to him. She had left him some time before. The young woman refused, and Lee, realizing he could not win her back with loving words, decided to try his luck with a .357-magnum.

Student Rosa Gonzalez, who was there, said: "The guy kept saying over and over, 'Just give me five minutes to talk to you, Carmen. Just give me five minutes.'

"But Carmen kept saying she didn't want to talk to him anymore. That everything was over between them, and that she was at the center to learn a skill and start a new life. That's when our teacher told the guy to leave."

And that's when Lee pulled a gun, sending teacher and some two dozen students stampeding toward the door.

Carmen never made it out with the others. Lee cornered her, waving the gun in her face. "Talk to me," he pleaded. "Just talk to me."

"I don't want to talk to you," the terrified woman said. "I don't want to talk to you ever again. It's over, Charles. What we had is over. Don't you realize that?"

The woman again tried to bolt for the door, but Lee sent a bullet crashing through a window in front of her, bringing Carmen to a stunned halt. The noise of the shot still ringing in her ears, she heard Lee say coldly, "Now, sit down. We'll talk."

The woman sat at a desk, desperately trying to control her fear. In a voice that quavered more than she had intended, she whispered, "All right, Charles, all right. What do you want to talk about?"

"Us," Lee said. "Carmen, we gotta talk about us, about our future."

Carmen Rojas knew there could be no future for her and Charles Lee—but she was not about to say that to a man who was threatening her life with a gun.

"Very well," she said. "We'll talk."

Minutes later, as the expert marksmen of the special weapons team set up in a building across from the training center, Police Captain Arthur Genero tried to negotiate with Lee, but the crazed gunman waved him away.

"I don't want to talk to you," Lee said. "I want to talk to Carmen. Now leave us alone."

Chief Victor Jacalone tried next, but Lee snarled, "Get away from me, or so help me I'll splatter her all over this room."

Helplessly, the police backed off. All they could do now was wait.

But, according to Passaic County Prosecutor Ronald Fava, one of the cops at the scene now recalled that Lee, who had worked as a bodyguard for several well-known celebrities and a security firm, knew Gerard Robbins from a black-belt karate class they shared.

"We decided then to ask Investigator Robbins to talk to the man," Fava says.

Robbins, in the understated way he has of recounting the story, says he "didn't ponder it any" when the call came in asking for his help.

"When I heard who it was, I knew I had to go down there and see what I could do," he says. "I knew Lee and had known him for a long time. I thought, Well, maybe I can talk to him."

Robbins arrived at the school shortly after 11 A.M., and Chief Jacalone laid it right on the line. "There's already been one shot fired. You walk into that classroom and you're entering a very dangerous situation. You'll be laying your life on the line, Robbins."

But the big investigator had already weighed the risks, and said he was willing to take his chances.

Robbins refused to wear a bulletproof vest. He also removed the comforting weight of his .38 special Smith and Wesson Model 60, loaded with 125-grain jacketed hollow-points, and handed it to a woman who was standing in the hallway outside the classroom.

"I hope I'll be back for this," he said, smiling.

"The Model 60 is a snub, a detective's gun, and maybe I could have carried it concealed into the classroom," he says. "But a man like Charles Lee, who's worked in security, knows guns and holsters, shoulder holsters, ankle holsters, other kinds of holsters. He could tell by the way I walked if I was carrying. I decided not to take a chance.

"Besides, the situation was very tense, but I felt it was under control. I said to myself, 'Maybe we can get through this thing without anybody getting hurt.'

"I went to the door of the classroom and called to Lee, and I asked him if I could come in. He looked surprised to see me, and maybe a little happy, and he said, 'Okay.'

"I walked inside and sat down. Then all three of us sat down, and Lee kept cocking and uncocking that big magnum, pointing the gun first at me and then at Carmen and then back again at me."

Lee nodded toward the scared woman. "She refuses to talk about us," he said. "She says it's all over between us. I just can't believe that."

"Things can always work out, if you handle them right," Robbins said. "We have to sit down and talk calmly. You can't do it with a gun in your hand. That just isn't the way. Give me the gun and we'll talk this thing through, all three of us. Maybe get some coffee and just talk."

"She says it's all over between us," Lee said again. "I can't accept that. I can't let that happen to us."

Robbins says: "It was about then I thought to myself, 'Jesus, Gerard, what have you gotten yourself into now?' "

The big cop realized in those first few seconds that he had a tiger by the tail, and that the situation could explode into murderous violence at any second. He knew that Carmen's life was on the line, a very thin line, and his was also. But he had no way of knowing that he was destined to hold tight to that line for the next, endless thirty minutes.

"The man sitting in that chair didn't even look like the Charles Lee I'd known for almost twelve years," Robbins says. "His hair was matted and his eyes were wild. When a man's in a state like that, you just can't tell what he's going to do. It's like he's on edge, and you can't second-guess him.

"I didn't think he was going to shoot. I figured if he planned to pull the trigger, he would have done that right off. But I still worried about the gun. He was easing the hammer up and down, and I badly wanted him to take his finger off the trigger. I didn't think he would shoot me, but accidents do happen. If the hammer slipped . . . well, there were SWAT teams on the roof and armed officers in the hallway and all hell could have broken loose."

Lee continued to babble, one second pleading with Carmen, the next threatening. The man was dangerously mentally unstable, continually working the action of the gun in his hand, the *click, click, click* of the cocking and uncocking hammer very loud in the stillness of the classroom.

Just as a cop who's survived a gunfight looks down at his piece and sees that it's smoking hot and the slide is slammed back and fifteen rounds are gone, yet can't remember once pulling the trigger, so Robbins has only sketchy memories of that harrowing half hour. He would later try to reconstruct them in his memory, painfully putting the jumbled pieces together like a nightmarish jigsaw puzzle.

"I do remember we talked and talked about Carmen," he says. "I knew Lee really loved her, but it had been over between them for a long time. She had been afraid of him for a long time before that, and finally all that pent-up fear made her leave him. He thought that things had been resolved between them and that she was leaving him for no reason. He loved her as much as a man can love a woman, I guess, and he didn't know what else to do.

"But I kept telling him that this wasn't the way. 'I know

you love her and want her back,' I said. 'But this isn't the way to do it. Not with a gun. It just isn't worth it . . .' "

And so it went, the controlled, careful talk going on and on as the clock approached noon. But in the quiet of the classroom it seemed that time was standing still, so that for Robbins and the wide-eyed, terrified Carmen Rojas each passing moment was freeze-framed in its own eternity, marked only by the metronome . . . *click* . . . *click* . . . *click* . . . as Lee worked his gun, the cylinder smoothly rotating as the hammer rose and dropped, rose and dropped, chamber by chamber, onto the bright brass and silvery percussion caps of the slim, devastating .357 rounds.

Yet it was the fall of that hammer that gave Robbins the time he needed to save the life of Carmen Rojas—and the life of Charles Lee.

The big investigator, trained in the disciplines of karate, had the physical and mental conditioning that every lawman needs if he is to survive in the streets, the conditioning that in a lethal confrontation often means the difference between life and death.

Robbins watched as Lee once again lowered the hammer of his revolver, his finger momentarily coming off the trigger, and knew he had maybe half a second to make his move.

"I just lunged forward and grabbed the gun," he said. "And we struggled. I yelled to the cops outside, 'For God's sake get in here!' But Lee suddenly quit struggling and started to hug me. Then he started to cry. I just held him in my arms till the others came and took him away."

■   ■   ■

It was over.

Prosecutor Fava said later: "There is no other way to describe the actions of Investigator Robbins but heroic."

That sentiment was echoed by the Policeman's Benevolent Association of New Jersey. PBA Awards Committee representative Charles Y. Taylor wrote:

"On Monday, March 19, 1990, at approximately 12:30 P.M., Gerard E. Robbins . . . distinguished himself in the City of Passaic, New Jersey.

"During this time period, his professional skill, knowledge and leadership saved three lives.

"This forceful act and alert versatility is an invaluable asset to the Prosecutor's Office of Passaic County. The distinctive accomplishments of County Investigator Robbins reflect credit upon himself and the law enforcement community of the State of New Jersey."

Later Robbins was inducted into the New Jersey Police Honor Legion, the New York Police Department Honor Legion and the New York Transit Police Honor Legion.

He was also to see Charles Lee, a man he considered a friend, sentenced to twelve years in prison.

"I will always consider the Charles Lee I knew for eighteen years to be a friend," Robbins said recently. "The Charles Lee I saw in that classroom was a different person. He was not the man I had known."

Despite the honors heaped on him, Gerard Robbins is still a modest man, a man who knows that in the field of law enforcement there are seldom clear-cut winners and losers.

"It's hard to feel good about what happened that day in March 1990," he said. "In the end, nobody is winning, and everybody is hurting.

"It would have been better for me, for Carmen Rojas, for Charles Lee himself, if he had never gone near that school."

But the inescapable fact is that some good did come out of it. One of the reasons Gerard Robbins entered law enforcement was to become a role model for others.

In that, he has surely succeeded.

OFFICER KATHERINE HELLER
U.S. Parks Police, Washington, D.C.

■■■■■■■■■■■■■■■■■■■■■■■

Never underestimate a woman. Renegade rogue Russell Baits did—and it cost the would-be cop killer and all-round bad guy his life.

The woman in question was petite, bubbly, United States Park Policewoman Katherine P. Heller, who proved that great courage often comes in very tiny packages. Officer Heller's bravery and decisiveness earned her the 1990 Police Officer of the Year award, and must surely lay to rest any lingering doubts about the abilities of women in law enforcement and their effectiveness in combat situations.

The five-foot-three, 107-pound officer's appointment with destiny began on the rainy evening of February 22, 1990, about 7:30 P.M. in Lafayette Park, across from the White House, where thirty-year-old Heller was on foot patrol. The cold and drizzling rain had cleared the park of visitors, and only homeless vagrants hunched their shoulders against the keening wind and sought shelter under the skeletal trees, glancing up now and then at leafless limbs that seemed to be contorted in pain, as though despairing that the sunlight would ever come again.

But Kathy Heller is one of those special women who carry their own sunlight with them, and despite the inconvenience of

185

the bulky uniform raincoat that fell to her ankles and the errant raindrops that trickled from the back of her hat and found their way down her neck, the young officer was enjoying the cool-as-mint evening and the fresh, clean, winter smell of the park.

"I'd begun my shift at two o'clock that day, and had already made several tours of the park," Heller says. "I'd stopped now and then and talked to the park's year-round residents, the demonstrators and the homeless and the vagrants who live there, and I'd then gone into the little police building in the park, we call it The Lodge, to type up my report.

"I'd been in there a few minutes when Officer Scott Dahl stopped by with a package for me from my desk sergeant. I knew Scott quite well then, though in later months we came to know each other very much better as circumstances threw us together, so that today we're almost like brother and sister.

"Scott stayed for several minutes and then left. I walked outside shortly afterwards and saw Scott standing with one of the resident park vagrants. 'There's been an assault in the park!' Scott yelled. I went back into the lodge and got my notebook and my PR 24 aluminum nightstick—at that time I never went anywhere without that stick—and when I came outside again, I went over to the wounded vagrant.

"The man had a deep head wound, and he was staggering, barely able to stay on his feet. He pointed to another vagrant across the street and said, 'That guy just hit me with a brick.' "

Officer Heller did not recognize the assailant, later identified as twenty-four-year-old Russell Baits, a park regular and known troublemaker with a history of convictions and violent behavior. As she attended to the wounded man, Officer Dahl, a former Marine, went after Baits.

"The wounded vagrant had his hand over his head," Heller recalls. "I told him to take his hand away from his wound so I could see it. When he took his hand away, I saw that his hand was covered in blood and the wound in his head was gaping wide open.

" 'You've got a real bad cut there,' I told him. But the man just looked at me with his lifeless eyes and shook his head. 'It doesn't matter,' he said. 'I'm a Vietnam vet, and it really doesn't matter.'

" 'I have to get you an ambulance,' I told him. 'Your wound needs to be stitched up, and we don't have a lot of time to waste.'

"During training, a rookie officer is taught to always keep an eye on his partner, so I glanced over to where Scott was and saw that he was on the ground, on his back, with Baits on top of him. I immediately called Dispatch on my portable radio, giving my location and the code for a fight in progress.

"Scott was yelling, screaming for help, and I ran over there. Baits was right on top of him, forcing his thumbs into Scott's eyes, attempting to gouge them from their sockets. Scott was very fit and strong, but Baits had jumped him without warning, and Scott's long raincoat had gotten tangled up in his legs and he'd fallen with Baits on top of him.

"Scott was screaming, like he was in terrible pain, yelling, 'Get him off! Get him off!' I tried to pull the guy off Scott, but I wasn't strong enough, so I started to beat Baits on the head with my PR 24. You're trained to hit an assailant on the arms and legs with the stick, but I knew that would be totally ineffective. As it was, I hit Baits maybe three or four times before he even glanced up. Scott later told me he could hear the *whack! whack!* of the stick striking bone, so I was hitting the guy pretty hard.

"Baits just looked up at me, then he totally ignored me, going back to whatever he was doing to Scott, and Scott was down there screaming."

Heller swung her stick three more times. After her seventh hit on Baits's unprotected head, the man suddenly jumped up and backed away from Officer Dahl.

"Scott was still on the ground, all tangled up in his raincoat, and I made a grab for Baits," Heller recalls.

"During the struggle, Baits's T-shirt had all but come off, and when I made my grab for him it fell around his waist. When that happened, I saw that he was holding a revolver. All Baits had to do was move the muzzle of his gun a fraction of an inch in my direction and he could have killed me. I still had my stick in my right hand and had no time to grab for my own gun.

"I ran, I guess you could say dived, for cover, and I heard Scott yell, 'He's got my gun, Kathy! He's got my gun!'

"Baits was now armed with the same weapon I was carrying, a Smith and Wesson service revolver loaded with .38 Special hollowpoints.

"The nearest available cover I could find was a light pole, and I ducked behind it. I looked over and saw that Baits was stalking Scott around a parked car. Both of them went around the car twice, but at one point Baits stopped and looked at Scott through the car windows. He was smiling. It was a really evil, malicious smile, and there was no doubt in my mind, or in Scott's, that Baits intended to kill him.

"I moved from the light pole to an electrical box on the sidewalk which gave me more cover. As I did this, Scott stopped at the front of the parked car, and Baits stopped at the rear right fender."

During his stalk of Officer Dahl, Baits had ignored Officer Heller and seemed totally unconcerned with her whereabouts. The man knew her nightstick had been ineffective and that she'd run for cover as soon as she'd seen his gun. Baits, a large, strong male, underestimated the tiny woman's courage and will to fight. It was to be a fatal mistake.

"Baits paid very little attention to me," Heller says. "It was as if I didn't even exist. I saw him raise his gun, pointing it at Scott, who immediately dived to the ground. I stepped out of my cover and closed the distance between me and Baits to about six to eight feet. Then I shot him.

"At first I thought I'd missed, because Baits didn't even flinch or glance in my direction. We'd been trained to double-tap, fire two fast rounds at the target, but for some reason I didn't use the double-tap. However, my mind still went into the training mode, and I thought, This man must go down. And I shot again. My second round hit Baits in the heart, and he went down.

"But the man was still moving, crawling on the grass, and Scott ran over and pushed Baits's arms above his head so that we knew where his hands were. Scott kept asking, 'Where's the gun? Where's the gun?' He was running around, trying to find it. Then a Metropolitan Police officer drove up in a cruiser, and Scott told him there had been a shooting. This officer helped with Baits, and Scott found his gun underneath the man's body.

"At this point I still had my gun aimed at Baits. I don't know how long I stood there like that. But then my sergeant came up to me, and I said, 'I shot him.' The sergeant nodded, took the gun out of my hands and told me it was all over. After that I went into deep shock and could remember nothing else."

Heller later learned that her first bullet had hit Baits in the pelvis. Her second round tore through the man's aorta, the great artery, springing from the left ventricle of the heart, that supplies blood to the entire body. Baits could not survive such a devastating wound, and he died later at the hospital.

"In the weeks and months that followed Baits's death, I more and more realized that law enforcement is a serious business," Heller says. "When you pin on a badge and strap on a gun, you're not playing a game. It's a serious, lifetime commitment you're making. It's not a job for clowns. A lot of people, a lot of cops, get on the job and they want to be involved in a shooting. They see it as the ultimate test of the police officer, a dangerous and necessary rite of manhood. I never thought that way. In fact I had been nicknamed 'The Social Worker Cop' and 'Officer Friendly,' and I always thought I'd be the last person in the world to drop the hammer on a man.

"You've heard of post traumatic stress disorder, a mental condition that often affects police officers after they've been forced to kill a man. Well, I had the worst case of that you can imagine. After the shooting I had psychiatric therapy twice a week and group therapy once a week, and without that help I doubt that I would have ever been able to return to duty.

"The psychiatric care I received was the best, but it didn't compare in effectiveness to the group therapy sessions. No one could understand where I'd been, what I was feeling, unless they'd been there themselves. Most of the officers in the group therapy sessions had not killed a man. They had wounded someone or had been shot themselves. When you wound somebody, they eventually get up and walk away, so the officer doesn't have the really deep guilt and responsibility feelings. But when you kill a man, it's final. There's no reversal. He's never going to get up and walk away.

"I needed to feel that I could handle the responsibility of Baits's death. And I needed to feel that Scott Dahl wasn't angry with me because he might feel I hadn't done enough. As it happened Scott was at the group therapy sessions, and he thought I was angry at him because I might think that he'd put me in a no-win situation.

"The group therapy sessions brought Scott and me much closer, a brother-and-sister relationship that has grown stronger with every passing day. It was a bad time in my life then. I had no doubt in my mind that I had done the right thing in killing Baits. But the stress of that shooting just turned my life upside down and shook it, so that it seemed like it was coming apart. I guess you could say that I was the classic post-traumatic-stress-syndrome patient. It was only the care, compassion and understanding of my psychiatrists and fellow officers that helped me through it."

Officer Kathy Heller returned to duty after ten weeks of intensive psychiatric therapy. She was offered limited duty when she returned, but loved police work so much that she turned it down. She asked instead to be assigned to the city's tough Anacostia district, which she still patrols in a cruiser.

Heller's heroism came as no surprise to the people who worked with her. In 1989 she'd ranked sixth out of 350 patrol officers on the Parks Police Force in making criminal felony arrests.

"Captain Hugh C. Irwin, her former lieutenant, says that Kathy Heller has what many other female officers possess—an instinctive ability to defuse tense situations. "You can *talk* somebody into handcuffs," he says. "When you acknowledge your limitations, you can beat almost anything."

In early 1990 Parks Police Assistant Chief Robert Langston called Heller at her home. "Kathy, are you ready for another shock?" he asked.

Officer Heller took a deep breath and said, "I guess I can handle it."

Gently, carefully, Langston said, "*Parade* magazine and the International Association of Chiefs of Police want to make you Police Officer of the Year. I won't advise you one way or the other. The decision must be yours." The Chief was handling his officer with kid gloves. He feared, as did many of his colleagues, that the award might bring back the very memories that Kathy had spent the past several months trying to forget.

But Kathy Heller had now come to terms with what had happened. She had spent many weeks in her own private hell, but she had emerged from it all the stronger and more committed than ever to her career in law enforcement.

"Chief Langston," she said, "I'd be honored."

In addition to being named Police Officer of the Year, Heller received numerous other awards, including a Medal of Honor from the Federal Law Enforcement Officers Association, a Medal of Honor from the United States Department of the Interior and a Police Officer of the Year award from the International Association of Women Police.

United States Parks Police Chief Lynn Herring sees Kathy Heller as a shining example to the other young women of this nation. "I hope her example will encourage young women everywhere to make the leap into law enforcement," she says.

"I believe police work to be a wonderful career for any woman," Heller says. "Women are proving their worth in law enforcement every day."

Kathy Heller, the eldest of five sisters, sought high adventure when she was growing up within the walls of her Potomac, Maryland, bedroom. She read Jack London and Alastair MacLean and loved Louis L'Amour westerns with their laconic, lantern-jawed heroes.

"I had lessons in piano and voice, but I wanted to break free," she says. "I was a wild spirit. I wanted to be out there on the ocean like Sea Wolf, pirating fat merchant ships.

"But growing up I didn't get that chance. My mother wouldn't even let me play sports for fear I'd get hurt."

Perhaps the highest tribute paid to this highly-decorated police officer comes from Scott Dahl, who says simply: "I wouldn't be here today if it weren't for Kathy. She saved my life."

Today, Officer Heller, who is unmarried, looks to her future, not to her past, yet she says: "As a police officer you live on the edge. I went over the edge and I was able to come back.

"But I can never again be the same person I was."

IN THE LINE OF DUTY . . .

OFFICER RICHARD MILLER
Baltimore City Police Department

■■■■■■■■■■■■■■■■■■■■■

On the afternoon of June 12, 1986, Officer Dick Miller was directing traffic outside Baltimore's Memorial Stadium. This was a regular detail for the thirty-one-year police veteran, and he loved the Orioles baseball team. Dick had many friends among the players, and his wife Betty even found a picture of Dick with Orioles star Brooks Robinson in his wallet after his death.

Officer Miller loved his work so much, he'd even passed up his scheduled retirement.

"When are you going to take that retirement?" Betty once asked him.

Dick thought on that for a while, then replied, "Honey, I think I'll do one more season with the Orioles."

He was never to get that chance.

Dick was directing traffic on Thirty-third Street at around six o'clock that June evening when a call came over his radio. "Stop the little white car," the officer said.

Neither he nor Dick Miller knew that the driver of the white car had already tried to run over Officer Michael Parks, and that Leonard Cirincione, the man at the wheel, was high on the hallucinogenic drug PCP.

Officer Miller and fellow officer Paul Aries went out into

the street and tried to flag down the car. The driver accelerated toward them. "He's not stopping!" Aries yelled. "Let's bail out."

The two cops ran to the opposite side of the street, standing behind some traffic cones. But Cirincione deliberately turned his car to the left, swerving through the cones to get at the lawmen. The car sideswiped Paul Aries but slammed full-force into Dick Miller, the 55 mph impact throwing him in the air, imbedding his glasses in the car's hood.

As Officer Miller's shattered body lay bleeding in the street, Cirincione claimed the whole thing was just a little accident. He continued to make that claim in the coming months, an attitude that enraged Paul Aries so much his fellow officers had to struggle to keep him away from the suspect.

Dick Miller's right leg was amputated at the Baltimore Shock-Trauma Unit a few hours after the accident. Betty was allowed to see her husband after the operation, but he was still heavily sedated.

"He didn't look like himself," she says. "All the bones in his face were broken, and they had a tube in his throat to keep him breathing. He had also suffered brain damage, but we didn't know how much."

Betty maintained a vigil by her husband's bedside, willing him to live. "I held his eyes open with my fingers and I'd talk to him," she says. "If I told him to squeeze my hand, he would do it sometimes, and sometimes he wouldn't."

Betty once brought a photograph of their granddaughter and held it up to Dick's eyes. He stared at it for a long time, then he squeezed her hand. Tears were rolling down his cheeks.

A big, robust man, Officer Dick Miller took a long time to die.

He suffered kidney and liver failure, then the seizures began. By Sunday, July 13, the seizures were coming every forty seconds, racking the big cop's tortured body, but still the ordeal dragged on.

Dick's daughter Pat asked her mother, "Mom, why can't he die?"

"I can't answer that," Betty said. "But I don't think we'll have long to wait for an answer."

Officer Dick Miller died on Monday, July 21, at 3:05 A.M., thirty-nine days after Leonard Cirincione ran him down. It was one day short of his thirty-second anniversary as a policeman.

Dick was given a hero's funeral, and thousands of officers attended from all over the nation. The baseball players from the Orioles team were also there to pay their last respects.

Today a plaque in Dick's memory can be seen at Memorial Stadium. It hangs there with just two others, one in honor of Baltimore Colts great Johnny Unitas and the other in honor of Dick's good friend Brooks Robinson.

The trial of twenty-nine-year-old Cirincione was an ordeal for the Miller family. The part-time construction worker had a history of drug abuse, and testified that he'd smoked "seven or eight joints" of PCP on the day he killed Officer Miller. Cirincione, who had twice previously been arrested for assaulting police officers, showed no remorse during his trial, and his family said they "couldn't understand what all the fuss was about." They even made an obscene gesture at the Miller family in the courtroom, and Leonard's father stated on a radio talk show that Officer Miller's death "was just an accident."

A furious Betty Miller called the radio station the next day. "Mr. Cirincione," she said on the air, "your son killed my husband. He destroyed my life. I ask you to look in the mirror and see me. I'm like you. You're lonely, but I'm lonely too. At least you have the option of going down to the

Maryland State Penitentiary to hug your son and make sure he's okay. My children and I visit the cemetery."

Cirincione was convicted of the first degree murder of Officer Richard Miller, and the first degree attempted murder of Officer Aries. He is currently serving a sentence of life plus twenty years at the Maryland State Penitentiary.

Betty Miller now helps the survivors of other officers who have lost their lives in the line of duty.

"If you can reach out and help someone, you get on with your life," she says. "You'll never get the answer to 'Why?' But you can go on."

DETECTIVE LEO JELLISON
New Hampshire State Police

■ ■

Let Gainesville, Florida, Police Lieutenant Sadie Darnell tell you something about evil. How it feels. How it stinks. How it can take the ordered fabric of your life and twist it, turn it, wrench it, till ordinary things become extraordinary and reality, if you let it, can lead you on a slow descent into madness.

"It was a much different murder scene than I had ever experienced before," she says of the 1991 Gainesville student slayings, speaking just a few days after she'd discovered the first two bodies.

"I was only in there maybe ten or fifteen minutes, but it seemed much longer. It was like I was absorbing things in slow motion, because there was so much at a sensory level to absorb.

"It was an eerie feeling and very much a feeling of the presence of evil.

"That all sounds so trite, I know, but it was a feeling I had never had before.

"The only thing that could have caused that . . . was something that was evil."

We will not consider the Gainesville slayings in these pages. But we will talk of evil, and a thing that was the very personification of evil. This thing walked upright and talked like a man. But he carried the gagging stench of the darkest reaches of hell in his heart.

The name of this creature was Christopher Wilder.

We will also learn that evil can not stand against good, that one good man is worth an infinite number of Wilders. The good in this case will be in the person of a big, laughing, huggy-bear of a cop named Leo "Chuck" Jellison. It was Jellison, fair, compassionate and valorous lawman that he is, who finally ended the career of Wilder, one of the most vicious, soul-less and sadistic serial killers in criminal history.

This is a book about heroes, and our purpose here is to honor Leo Jellison. But to appreciate the bravery of this fine officer, we must first relate the story of Christopher Wilder, in all its shocking brutality. We sincerely ask the forgiveness of the more gentle reader, who will surely find the telling of it upsetting in the extreme.

■   ■   ■

Christopher Bernard Wilder was born on March 13, 1945, in Australia, the result of a union between a United States Navy career man who reached the rank of warrant officer, and a Sydney girl he met during World War II.

Wilder was the eldest of three sons, and his earliest memories were of being shuttled back and forth from Australia to the United States till the restless family finally settled in New South Wales, where the elder Wilder, now retired from the Navy, established a hardware business.

Young Christopher was a whining, difficult infant, colicky and cranky, and so sickly that at one point he was given the last Rites of the Catholic Church. A couple of years later he almost drowned in a swimming pool, and at age three he took sick again and almost died.

By the time he was a teenager, the kid had major
problems—all of them in his head.

Shortly after Wilder's seventeenth birthday, he and three
of his buddies were arrested for the brutal gang rape of a girl
on an isolated beach. Young Christopher spent a few days in
jail and then pleaded guilty in a juvenile court to a reduced
charge of unlawful carnal knowledge. He was given a year's
probation that included mandatory counseling—and electroshock treatments.

The painless shock treatments terrified young Wilder. He
believed the doctors were doing something terrible to his
brain, and he vowed he would never go through an
experience like that again.

He married at twenty-three, but the ill-starred union
lasted only a few days, his distraught bride complaining that
"Christopher only wanted unnatural sex . . . There was a
lot of sexual abuse." She also said Wilder kept a collection
of women's underwear in the trunk of his car, along with
dozens of photographs of topless bathing beauties.

A reporter for the *Miami Herald* wrote years later: "Early
on, there was a suggestion that he was a snow dropper, a guy
who steals ladies' clothes off clotheslines. The wife found
some in her house. Clothes that weren't hers."

In November 1969, Wilder was posing as a professional
photographer. He was fit and tanned and wore a thin gold
chain around his neck, and he had discovered that he had the
ability to make female hearts flutter.

He talked a naive, nineteen-year-old student nurse into
posing naked at a beach a few miles from Sydney, promising, "Once the agencies get a look at these pictures, honey,
you'll be one of Australia's top models in a matter of
weeks."

But Wilder had other things on his mind.

He later told the hysterical girl that he would mail copies
of the lurid photographs to the hospital where she worked

unless she agreed to have sex with him. He made it plain that he was talking about Wilder's brand of sex. Crude, unnatural and violent.

The girl refused and went to the police. She later failed to press charges, but Wilder knew he was on record. He was a marked man, and he knew that some tough, big-bellied Australian cops were praying he'd make a wrong move.

But he didn't. He fled to South Florida, to the land of sunshine, beaches . . . and thousands of golden, long-legged girls.

With hindsight, how readily that chilling line from Shakespeare springs to mind, as though the bard had written it with Christopher Wilder in mind: "Something wicked this way comes . . ."

The charmer with the twanging Aussie accent did well in the Sunshine State. He set himself up in the electrical contracting and construction business, and as Florida prospered in the booming late sixties and early seventies, so did Christopher Wilder.

He lived in a snazzy bachelor pad, complete with a floodlit indoor/outdoor pool and Jacuzzi. The pool had a map of Australia on the bottom, and the surrounding tiles sported pictures of koalas. Wilder was an animal lover. He shared his home with three show-quality English setters and regularly made donations to Save the Whales and the Seal Rescue Fund. He braked for turtles and armadillos.

Dozens of beautiful girls paraded in and out of his house, lounged around the pool or drove with him in his Cadillac Eldorado convertible or his customized Porsche 911. He wore gold chains around his thick neck, gold ID bracelets on his wrists, diamond pinkie rings that flashed in the Florida sun.

Christopher Bernard Wilder was living the American Dream—and was about to turn it into a nightmare.

At this stage in his life Wilder was a sexually dysfunc-

tional pervert, a product of his restless childhood and the
electroshock treatments he'd received at age seventeen. He
considered himself a superior human being and that the rest
of humanity, especially females, was created solely for his
pleasure. He was incapable of a healthy sexual relationship
with a woman and treasured pornography and the lurid
covers of detective magazines that show terrified girls
menaced by knives or guns. His motive for murder was
simple: sexual gratification. Torture, terror and murder
aroused him, fed the evil that had been spawned and then
continued to grow strong within him. He killed merely to
live out his own diseased fantasies. He was, by any
standard, a monster.

In March 1971, Wilder was arrested in Pompano Beach
for trying to talk young girls into posing nude for him. He
pleaded guilty and was fined a few dollars.

Then, on September 9, 1976, he drove a beautiful,
miniskirted high school girl to a remote wooded area and
asked her to perform oral sex on him. When the sixteen-
year-old refused, Wilder slapped her, hard. "You're going to
suck it . . . You're going to do what I say or I'll kill you,"
he snarled.

The girl protested that she was a virgin. "I've never been
with a man before," she pleaded.

Wilder slapped the girl again. "You do as I say or you'll
never be with a man again," he said. "I'll leave you dead,
here and now, if you don't do what I tell you."

Sobbing, terrified, the teenager bent her head and did as
she was told.

Charges were brought, and Wilder was later taken into
custody. During his trial, clinical psychologist Dr. D. G.
Boozer told the court: "After psychiatric examination I have
determined that Wilder is a dangerous man. I strongly
recommend that he be placed in an institution."

A badly misled jury disagreed. They thought Christopher

Wilder was merely a nice young man who was misunderstood. He was acquitted.

In June 21, 1980, Wilder raped a teenager after telling her he was the representative of a famous modeling agency.

"He made his job a lot easier by spiking a pizza he bought for the girl with some kind of knockout drug," said one embittered police officer—after yet another sympathetic jury gave Wilder probation and recommended that he visit a psychologist for therapy.

Is it any wonder that this twisted, dangerous animal thought himself a superior human being, a man beyond the law, after such VIP treatment from misguided jurors?

Wilder visited Australia in 1982 and got himself into another scrape after he forced a pair of teenage girls to pose for pornographic pictures. His family posted a bond of $350,000 and the balding thirty-nine-year-old returned to Florida. But this time the cops wanted very badly to talk to him. They figured he might know a lot more than he was saying about the inexplicable disappearances of Orange Bowl Princess and budding model Beth Kenyon and lovely, vivacious Rosario Gonzales, who also wished to enter the glamorous world of the top fashion model.

Aware of his sick, sex-slave fantasies, Wilder's therapist also suspected that her patient knew more about Rosario's disappearance than he was telling. She asked him during one of their last counseling sessions to come clean.

Without batting an eyelid, Wilder replied, "I read about the poor girl in the paper. It's terrible, just terrible. But I know absolutely nothing about it."

But the Miami police were closing in, especially after a Coral Gables gas station attendant identified Wilder as the man he had seen with Beth Kenyon on the day she disappeared. On March 13, 1984, as an all-points bulletin was issued for the arrest of a "race car driver from Boynton

Beach." Wilder bought an eleven-year-old Chrysler New Yorker—and fled.

It was the beginning of a demonic cross-country odyssey of murder, rape, torture . . . and terrifying, screaming death.

Wilder, a sometime race driver, had competed in the Miami Grand Prix not long before his killing spree began, and some said his seventeenth place finish was what set him off. But the evil in Wilder had been festering for a long time. By any law of common sense, he should have been taken out of circulation years before. But that familiar story needs no further emphasis here.

Here is the full catalog of Wilder's horror journey, though some of the more sickening details have been omitted to spare the feelings of the more timid reader:

March 16, Indian Harbor, Florida: Beautiful, twenty-one-year-old Theresa Anne Wait is abducted from a shopping mall. Her mutilated body is later found floating in a creek. A Chrysler New Yorker, driven by a bearded, middle-aged man was reported seen in the area.

March 18, Tallahassee, Florida: A willowy, blond Florida State University student is approached by a bearded man with a camera slung around his neck as she shops at a local mall. The man tells her he's a fashion photographer and asks her to pose for him. Dazzled by the prospect of a modeling career, the girl readily agrees.

As the pair approach the man's New Yorker, he suddenly swings a roundhouse punch into the coed's stomach and follows up with a blow to her head. He then zips her into a sleeping bag and throws her in the trunk of his car.

The terrified nineteen-year-old is driven to Bainbridge, Georgia, where her brutal abductor carries her into a motel room, throws her on a bed, then unzips her from the sleeping bag.

During the ghastly hours that follow, Wilder strips the

girl, rapes her twice, then forces her to perform unnatural sex acts. He attaches an electric cord to her toes, and for two hours he giggles and hugs himself in his hilarity as he repeatedly racks her body with jolts of electricity.

The monster is highly amused, but there is worse to come. He has another sadistic torture in his grotesque bag of tricks.

Wilder welds the helpless coed's eyes shut with superglue, tunes into an aerobics program on TV—and forces her to dance naked for him.

The girl later manages to run into a bathroom, locks the door and screams for help. Wilder grabs his clothes and scampers, naked, to his car.

March 23, Beaumont, Texas: Dazzlingly beautiful wife and mother Terry Diane Walden, twenty-four, drops her daughter off at a day-care center, then drives to attend classes at nearby Lamar University. She never arrives.

Her starkly white body is later found floating in the murky waters of a canal dam. The dead woman is tightly bound with cords, and her mouth is taped shut. Her breasts are mutilated by three deep, vicious stab wounds made by a hunting knife.

Her grieving young husband says later: "The day before she disappeared, my wife told me that a bearded man had come on campus and asked her to pose for photographs. She told him to get lost and leave her alone."

Two weeks later a Beaumont policeman finds Wilder's New Yorker abandoned in a downtown parking lot . . . during that time three more women have been kidnapped, sexually abused, tortured . . . and savagely murdered.

By this time Wilder is a frightened, hunted animal. But he is deadly dangerous and will kill again and again and again.

March 25, Oklahoma City, Oklahoma: Twenty-one-year-old aspiring model Suzanne Wendy Logan is abducted from a shopping center. Her body is later found wedged into the roots of a cedar tree near Manhattan, Kansas, nearly three hundred miles away.

Her breasts are savagely bitten as though by a wild animal, and her back is pitted with hundreds of tiny puncture wounds, made by the point of a sharp hunting knife. The girl's beautiful blond hair has been crudely hacked off, as has her pubic hair. A single vicious thrust from the knife through her left breast finally ended her terrible torment.

Medical examiners say that Suzanne had been dead less than an hour when her body was found.

March 29, Grand Junction, Colorado: Young, beautiful Sheryl Bonaventura disappears from the Mesa Mall, where she works. A few hours before, another young woman was approached by a bearded man who asked her to model for him. She wasn't interested, but eighteen-year-old Sheryl dreams of being a model and has already posed for some fashion layouts. She readily agrees.

Her nude body is recovered from the Kanab River, a few miles across the Utah state line from Page, Arizona, on May 3, 1984, nearly three weeks after the death of her killer. She has been stabbed in the heart, shot, and her left breast has been terribly mutilated.

April 1, Las Vegas, Nevada: Michelle Korfman, the lovely, vivacious, seventeen-year-old daughter of a casino executive, leaves to compete in a modeling contest at a mall. She never returns home.

Police later find her 1982 Camaro, a gift from her father, parked behind Caesar's Palace. Amazingly, detectives also come up with a photo of Wilder, taken at the department store where the modeling contest was held. The photo shows the long, miniskirted legs of a young model . . . and looking between them is the intent, smug face of Christopher Wilder.

Some of the girls will later show up at the parking lot behind Caesar's Palace, lured there by the bearded man who offered them modeling assignments. But he never appears.

Michelle's badly decomposed corpse won't be found till a month after Wilder's death, in a national forest near Los Angeles. Her mouth will be full of dirt, and William E. Gold of the county coroner's office will say: "It's probable the deceased was forced facedown into the dirt at some point at or near her death."

The beautiful teenager was suffocated.

April 4, Santa Monica, California: Wilder wakes up at the Proud Parrot Motel in Torrance, a suburb of Los Angeles. At noon he drives to the nearby DelAmo shopping mall, where he meets sixteen-year-old Tina Marie Risico, a sexy little blonde described by her friends as "wild" and "a little strange."

Blue-eyed Tina Marie poses on the beach while Wilder snaps what he says is a roll of pictures for a billboard assignment. He promises to pay her a hundred-dollar modeling fee.

When the teenager looks at her watch and says, "It's time I was getting home," her bearded, kindly friend turns suddenly nasty. He pulls a gun and trusses her up with rope, snarling obscenities.

Wilder takes the girl to a motel in Prescott, Arizona, where he ties her to a bed and sexually abuses and tortures her for hours with a 110-volt cattle prod.

He next drives to Taos, New Mexico, with his prisoner in tow, and checks into another motel.

But the next morning Wilder gets a shock. The TV news tells him that he's been placed on the FBI's Most Wanted List. Two days later he gets another shock—TV stations are showing the video he made for a dating service three years before.

For the first time since he fled Florida, Christopher Wilder knows real fear. He simply can't believe that someone like himself, a special and very superior human being, could be shot on sight by some dumb bozo of a cop with a gun and a badge.

Gasping like a stranded fish, a terrified Wilder gulps back his terror and bundles Tina Marie into the car that had once belonged to Terry Walden and hits the road again. With himself at the wheel and Tina Marie beside him, he races across the country, moving farther and farther from the dragnet trying to catch him.

April 10, Merrillville, Indiana: Pretty sixteen-year-old Dawnette Sue Wilt is approached in the Southlake Mall by another teenager who introduces herself as Tina Marie Wilder. Moments later Tina Marie introduces Dawnette to a middle-aged, balding man who asks her if she would like to model for him. The teenager readily agrees to walk with Tina to the man's car to sign a model release form. But once she is there, Wilder pulls a gun and bundles Dawnette into the backseat. He then climbs on top of the terrified girl and rapes her brutally as Tina Marie drives.

The three drive across Indiana to Wauseon, Ohio, where Dawnette is dragged into a motel room, sexually abused and tortured with electric shocks.

Wilder, Tina Marie at his side, takes great pleasure in seeing the girl convulsively jerk and moan, her eyes screaming above her taped mouth as the relentless electricity hits. Now he knows he's getting even for all those electroshock treatments he endured in Australia so many years ago.

Revenge for Christopher Wilder is always sweet.

The next night the trio is in Niagara Falls, New York, where Dawnette is again raped and tortured. But Wilder is by now growing tired of her.

Next morning he forces Tina Marie to drive to Barrington, in the beautiful Finger Lakes region of the state, and once there he drags Dawnette into the woods. He orders the terrified girl to kneel, then plunges a knife into her back and chest. Wilder will never know it, but miraculously the teenager survives. After surgery, she is able to describe, in grotesque detail, what she has been through. On the pillow of her hospital bed is a Cabbage Patch doll, bought with donations from the sheriff's deputies. She picks up the doll and hugs it as the detectives leave.

April 13, Rochester, New York: Two hours after stabbing Dawnette, Wilder is with Tina Marie in a shopping mall—where he stalks his final victim.

Beth Ann Dodge is a thirty-three-year-old mom and a Sunday school teacher. She is on her way to meet friends for lunch in her 1982 Pontiac Trans-Am. Wilder knows the cops have a description of Terry Walden's Cougar. It's time to change cars, and he feels that Beth's sporty, dashing Trans-Am is tailor-made for a man like him.

Seconds after the woman steps out of her car at the Eastview Mall, she is confronted by Wilder, who shoves a gun into her ribs and snarls, "Get into my car."

With Tina Marie following in the gold Trans-Am, Wilder drives to a country road near a gravel pit. The woman, now terribly afraid, pleads for her life, telling Wilder that she has young children. But Wilder drags Beth from his car, roughly forces her to the ground and shoots her once in the back of the neck with his .357-magnum. The woman's body is found a few hours later, near the abandoned Cougar.

A police dragnet now spreads over upstate New York, but once again Wilder eludes his captors, and drives to Boston, where his fantasy world takes a bizarre twist.

He takes Tina Marie to Logan International Airport and buys her a ticket home to Los Angeles. Wilder tells her he doesn't want her to see him die. His last words to the girl are "All you gotta do, kid, is write a book."

Tina Marie will later recall that the moment was a tender one. "It was heartbreaking," she says. "It was so sentimental."

Once back in L.A., Tina goes shopping, where she uses

the wad of cash in her pocket to buy lingerie. She then goes to the house of a friend, who later accompanies her to the police station to tell her story.

A reporter visits Tina's mother the next day. She is a pretty blond woman in her thirties with a scorpion tattoo on her forearm and a silver ring circling one toe.

"Tina's out partyin'," she tells the stunned scribe. "I'm goin' out partyin' too."

The FBI later takes Tina Marie into custody, but releases her, saying she has been brainwashed by Wilder and is a victim, not an accomplice. Wilder did not allow the girl to change her clothes during the nine days he held her captive. She still seems to carry the killer's vile stench.

Psychiatrist Dr. Roland Summit of the University of California Medical Center says in a prepared statement for the press and police: "The girl was subjected to sexual humiliation and brainwashing. The pattern follows explicitly one in which terror and obedience are instilled in the victim."

After leaving the girl at the airport, Wilder drives out of Boston along Route 128 and tries to snatch one more love slave, a nineteen-year-old woman standing near her stalled car. But the teen eludes him and calls the police.

At one-thirty that afternoon, Wilder drives the Trans-Am into Vic's Getty Oil Station at the corner of Bridge and Main Streets in the village of Colebrook, New Hampshire, about ten miles from the Canadian border.

He doesn't know it, but he has just minutes to live. His nemesis, the tall, grim figure of thirty-three-year-old state detective Leo Jellison, is just a few yards away.

Jellison, a six-foot-three, 250-pound father of two young sons, has just finished lunch at the Speedy Chef restaurant. He and fellow officers Howard Weber and thirty-six-year-old Wayne Fortier, along with Colebrook Police Chief

Wayne Cross, are returning by unmarked cruiser to the town police station on Bridge Street.

As Wilder chats casually with gas station attendant Wayne Delong, Fortier spots a Trans-Am at Vic's that resembles one they received a bulletin on that morning.

"Hey!" the young trooper exclaims excitedly. "That looks like the car that Wilder guy is supposed to be driving."

Jellison eyeballs the Trans-Am. "Sure looks like it," he says. "Maybe I should stroll on over there and have a few words with the driver."

After dropping the others off on Bridge Street, Jellison and Fortier return to the station to confront the driver, who has just asked for the shortest route to the Canadian border.

Jellison, huge, implacable, his homely features impassive, approaches the man and says politely, "Excuse me, sir, I'd like to have a word with you."

Wilder looks startled. Then his jaw drops and a look of sheer terror crosses his face. He races quickly to his car and finds the passenger door is locked. He runs quickly around to the driver's side and dives for the .357-magnum in the glove box.

Jellison, young, fit, highly trained, could draw and fire his service revolver in something less than a half a second, killing the desperately fumbling fugitive. But he does not. He throws himself on Wilder, grasping the killer in a massive bear hug. Silently the men struggle for the sweat-slicked .357. A shot rings out, the bullet ripping into Jellison's chest. Another shot. This time the .357 slug, traveling at around 1,450 feet per second, slams into Wilder's heart. The organ explodes and the killer dies instantly. Wilder's finger is still on the trigger as Jellison lets go of him.

The big trooper, badly wounded, slumps in the front seat of the Trans-Am and whispers to Fortier, "Jesus, Wayne, I've been hit."

As Jellison is rushed to the Upper Connecticut Valley Hospital in Colebrook, curious sightseers crowd around the death car. Wilder has little dignity in death. He looks like a balding, fat rag doll. His cowboy boots have been removed, and his white, bare feet look grotesque as cops crowd around, looking for an identifying scar on his ankle.

After emergency surgery to remove the bullet from his chest, Leo Jellison wakes up to find Chief Cross holding his hand. The trooper grins weakly and says, "Jesus Christ, my chest feels like a train hit me."

■   ■   ■

Cross knew then that Jellison was going to be all right.

Wilder, that personification of everything evil and bad in humanity, the playboy who thought himself so unique, so superior, died a dog's death at the hands of a much better man.

He would have hated that.

In June, 1984, a fully recovered Detective Jellison and Trooper Fortier received an armful of framed awards, medals of valor and commendations from Governor John Sununu, the FBI, the state police and other law enforcement agencies.

In his acceptance speech at the statehouse in Concord, Jellison said: "I squeezed Wilder's arms together for what seemed an awful long time. I knew I was shot, and I was afraid I was going to get shot again."

Today, Leo Jellison is a captain in the New Hampshire State Police. When he visits Colebrook, as he occasionally does, he always draws a crowd of admirers, not because he ended the career of Christopher Wilder, but because the people of the town still remember him as a fair, honest and upright man, a true hero in every sense of the word.

"Even after he left Colebrook, he'd stop by for coffee and half the town would turn out to see him," Cross says.

Local gas station owner Mike Divney says: "He's a cop with a good sense of humor, and he's fair. Even the people he's nabbed like him."

Asked why he didn't simply draw his gun and shoot Wilder all those years ago, Jellison says: "I've had cops say to me, 'Hell, I'd have pulled my piece and blown the son of a bitch away.' Well, that is their way. It's not Leo Jellison's way.

"I was not Wilder's judge and executioner. It was my job, my duty, to capture him and see him brought to justice. As it happened, he did die. But that was all of his doing and none of mine."

At this writing, Rosario Gonzalez and Beth Kenyon have not yet been found. There is little evidence that the ordeal their families have been suffering for almost a decade will end anytime soon.

Wilder's brother claimed the killer's body, which was returned to Boynton Beach, Florida, for burial. Police made a plaster cast of Wilder's jaws and teeth so they could match it up with the bites on the breasts of his many victims.

The killer's brain was removed during the official autopsy in New Hampshire and kept for further study, in a bid to find the root source of its evil.

It has since vanished.

DETECTIVE CHRISTINE BRIDGES
Denver, Colorado, Police Department

■■■■■■■■■■■■■■■■■■■■■

Detective Christine Bridges lay very still on the bed and watched the shadow of the bedroom window, cast by the glow of the street lamp outside, slant like a surreal tic-tac-toc game across the wall to her left. She quietly brought her watch up close to her eyes and glanced at the time. It was a few minutes after ten.

"Maybe he isn't coming," she thought, "maybe not to-night."

It didn't surprise her. Stakeouts like this seldom worked. All those long hours of tedious waiting and watching . . . and at the end of the day you always came up empty-handed. Well, that wasn't quite true. Maybe once in a thousand tries the cops got lucky and the bad guy entered the trap.

"But not tonight," Christine told herself again. "I've got a funny feeling that this is one trap that won't be sprung."

A few minutes later the young cop realized just how wrong she'd been. Her body stiffened, every muscle tense, as she stared at the angled rectangles of the shadow on the wall. A man's arm, the shape distorted and huge, slowly crept upward from the darkness beneath the reflection of the window. The arm clenched into a fist, which silently and with psychotic patience gradually began to inch the window upward . . .

Christine felt a sudden spasm of excitement in her

stomach. She tightened her grip on the butt of her Smith and Wesson Chief's Special .38, finding comfort in the familiar feel of checkered walnut and steel.

The man at the window, the man known as the Ski-Mask Rapist, the man who had terrorized the city of Denver for the past two years, now had the window open more than a foot. Silently, carefully, he crawled through this gap and into the bedroom.

That night, Frank Vargas wanted the young, attractive woman on the bed. He wanted her badly. She would be his twenty-third victim.

He didn't know it yet, but he was about to make the biggest mistake of his life . . .

■   ■   ■

"I volunteered for that stakeout in February 1986, about a week before I was due to get married," thirty-four-year-old Christine says.

"The premise was simple. I'd set myself up as a decoy, try to lure the rapist into the bedroom, and then nail him. Nobody really gave the plan much chance of succeeding.

"Frank Vargas, who was first known as the Gentleman Rapist and later the Ski-Mask Rapist, had no prior criminal record before he was arrested. He had one traffic ticket for speeding, and that was it. He was described as a model citizen, an ordinary, hardworking guy. Yet he raped twenty-two women, of all ages, before we arrested him.

"When the rapes first began, he had the reputation of being gentle with his victims, that's why he got the name the Gentleman Rapist. But as the crimes went on, and the number of his victims grew, he was becoming progressively more violent. As the violence escalated, he started to beat women, often badly, when they didn't comply. He always carried a weapon—a knife, gun or a hammer—though as far as we know, he never used a weapon on any of the women he attacked.

"The increasing pattern of violence can be seen in a case where he didn't employ his usual method of climbing through the victim's bedroom window at night, but waited for the woman in her hallway. He followed the woman inside her apartment, and when she walked into the living room, Vargas just slammed her in the face, threw her to the floor and raped her.

"That was the last rape he committed before we caught him."

Christine had just been transferred from the Vice Squad to the Burglary Detail, when she was asked to volunteer for a stakeout that might net the ruthless rapist. Alarmed by the man's increasing tendency to violence, and worried about all the negative media publicity, the Denver city fathers pressured the police to pull out all the stops and catch the Ski-Mask Rapist before he struck again.

"My sergeant knew of an apartment where the window had been tampered with, but where the rapist had failed to gain entry," Christine recalls. "He thought the man might return to try again, and asked me if I'd like to become a decoy and spend the night there.

"I said, 'Sure!' I'd just come from the Vice Squad, where I'd worked undercover a lot, and this job sounded a lot more interesting than investigating burglaries.

"The apartment in question was in the Washington Park area of Denver, right in the middle of where most of the attacks had happened. We called this the yuppie area of town. There are a lot of apartments there, and a lot of big homes that have been divided up into apartments. It's an expensive area to live in, but it's close to Denver University, so a lot of college girls live around there."

According to Detective Bridges, the Ski-Mask Rapist operated mostly in this area, though he did not exclusively target young college students. On one occasion he tried to attack a woman in her seventies, but this legally armed senior citizen drew her weapon and Vargas scampered.

"However, most of his victims were young, single women," Christine says. "He later refused to talk about any of the women he'd attacked, so he never stated if he had any age or appearance preference.

"The only connection Vargas had with the area was a bar where he used to hang out. This bar was right at the edge of the Washington Park area, and he might have operated from there.

"The apartment where the stakeout was set up was one half of a duplex, converted from a house that was built in the late 1800s. The girl who lived in the other side had been raped and moved out. Then another girl moved in with her boyfriend. This young couple were lying asleep in bed one night when Vargas, wearing his ski mask, walked into their bedroom. He had come back to rape the same girl, but was surprised by another girl being in there with her boyfriend.

"The couple chased him off, and later found that he'd cut the phone lines to the entire duplex.

"After this report got out, the girl living next door got spooked. She was terrified, thinking she might be the rapist's next victim, and refused to spend another night in her part of the duplex. She went home that evening after school to get some clothes, planning to move in with her boyfriend. That's when she heard a noise at her bedroom window.

"She called for the police, and when the officers arrived, they found that the phone lines had again been pulled away from the wall, though Vargas hadn't managed to cut them. A hole had also been cut in a glass pane of the window, so someone could just reach in and unlock it.

"This incident was reported to the Burglary Detail as an attempted break-in. My sergeant was aware of all the rapes taking place in the area and saw a pattern emerging. That's when he had the bright idea of putting someone in the abandoned apartment as a decoy. He figured the rapist would come back."

Asked if the assignment scared her, Detective Bridges says, "Nah.

"It's not that I'm tough or particularly brave," she explains, "but in police work you take part in so many of these surveillance things, and they never fly, they never happen. You spend hours and hours sitting there, trying to catch somebody, and it just doesn't happen. It's always a bust.

"In the Vargas case, we just got really lucky. You know, the first night that we're there, the guy shows up. It was a million-to-one shot.

"A lot of these guys, serial rapists, are window peepers. They'll go to the window every night, often for weeks, keeping track of their victims, making sure they are always there at a certain time. This way, when they finally do attack, they feel they have more control over the situation. I think Vargas had been there, peeping night after night, and the girl was never there. She'd gone to stay with her boyfriend. When I got in the apartment, he peeped again and thought, Oh good, she's back, and decided to attack."

On the night of the stakeout Christine got to the apartment at around five-thirty in the evening. It was bitterly cold, a tattered wind blowing wet flakes of snow around the eaves of the building, pushing icy fingers into every nook and cranny of the brickwork. The moon appeared now and again from behind scudding clouds, casting pale shadows on the damp sidewalk. A few leafless trees raised bare, skinny arms to the sky and seemed to shiver in the biting breeze.

"I arrived at the duplex in a rented car that was just like the car owned by the girl who'd lived in the apartment," Christine says. "I took groceries in there, cooked dinner, then just hung out and watched some TV. I made it real obvious I was there, turned on all the lights and everything. What a woman wears means nothing to a rapist, so I didn't have to dress provocatively or anything like that. It was cold, so I was wearing jeans and a sweatshirt, for comfort's sake."

Christine wasn't quite alone. Another officer, Detective Dave Pontarelli, spent five uncomfortable hours hiding in the bedroom closet, "a real little closet at that," according to Christine, while other officers were scattered around the area, well away from the house.

"Vargas had been so lucky in the past, we didn't want him to see anyone close to the house," Christine says. "It would be obvious to him that he was being set up.

"Dave and I had already set up a plan of action. We knew we'd have to pull our guns on this guy for sure, and didn't want to get into a crossfire situation. We had it so that if he came to the left side of the bed, I'd roll to my right while Dave came crashing out of the closet. If he came to the right, I'd roll to my left and so on. And, the perfect situation, if he came to the foot of the bed, I could roll one way and Dave could come out of the closet, so we could cut off any escape to the door or the window.

"Well, as I was saying, I'd eaten dinner and I was just hanging out watching TV. I watched 'Miami Vice' because I'd never seen it before. I remember looking at the screen and thinking, 'Do people really think cops live like that, dressed in designer fashions, driving around in Jaguars?' I've never even been in a Jaguar in my life. A cop's wages don't run to that kind of luxury.

"But as I sat there watching those wealthy cops on TV, I got the uneasy feeling I was being watched. You know that feeling you get when someone is watching you . . . it makes you feel like your skin is crawling, like eyes are sliding like slugs all over your body.

"I got up slowly, stretched and pretended to yawn. I walked into the bedroom and whispered to Dave Pontarelli through the closet door: 'I think he's out there, Dave. I think he's watching me.'"

From the closet, Officer Pontarelli's muffled whisper said, "Go to bed. Pretend like you're turning in for the night. But be careful. Stay alert."

Because Vargas always attacked his victims in the dark, Christine turned out all the lights. She then got into bed.

"I didn't want to cover myself with the sheet for fear I might get tangled up in it when the time came to move, so I just spread my coat over me," she recalls.

The young cop lay there for almost thirty minutes, her ears straining to catch every sound, hearing only the wind sighing around the building, whispering through the trees. Maybe after all this the Ski-Mask Rapist wasn't coming! Christine turned her head on the pillow and watched the shadow of the bedroom window as it angled across the wall. A few more minutes slowly ticked past.

Then she saw a man's arm appear . . .

∎   ∎   ∎

"It was real eerie," she says. "Because of the shadow cast by the street lamp, his arm looked huge. I saw this huge arm come up and start to unlock the window. He did it very slowly and very silently.

"By this time I was so excited, I wanted to jump up and grab him. But I knew I'd have to lay there and pretend I was asleep until he came into the bedroom. Remember when you were a kid and your mother would come into your room and you'd pretend to be asleep but your eyes weren't really closed all the way? Well, that's what I did that night.

"I watched him from under my eyelashes, and it seemed to take him forever to crawl through the window. He made no noise at all, and if I'd really been asleep I would have never known he was there.

"Dave was in the closet, but I had no way of telling him that the rapist was here. I couldn't even whisper because I didn't want to scare the guy away.

"I watched the shadow on the wall, seeing the window open inch by inch. I felt a cold breeze as the window opened wider. I saw the Ski-Mask Rapist put one leg through the open window. Then the other. He was silent, like a cat. He was in the bedroom. He moved away from the window. I could hear him breathing softly behind the mask as he quietly padded across the carpeted floor.

"Then he came to the foot of the bed, the perfect place, just like we'd planned. The rapist slowly eased himself onto the bed, one careful leg at a time. Then he kneeled down on the bed, a hammer in his right fist. Again I could hear that soft, silent breathing, the only sound in the stillness of the room.

"Then all hell broke loose!

"At that instant Dave kicked open the closet door. It sounded like a shotgun going off because it had been so deathly quiet before. Dave kicked open the door, and I rolled to my left, onto the floor. We had him. He couldn't go anywhere.

"When the closet door opened with such a crash, Vargas jumped about a mile in the air. He was terrified. One second he thinks he's about to rape some sleeping young girl, the next he's looking at two guns pointed at his head.

"Vargas threw his hands up in the air and wailed, 'Don't shoot me! Oh, please, don't shoot me!' He was crying, sobbing, begging for the mercy he had never shown any of his victims.

"He was just a little yellow wimp, like all of these guys are. We put the cuffs on him and pulled off his little ski mask. Tears were rolling down his cheeks. He was crying all the time, begging us not to shoot him."

Without even trying to disguise her contempt and disgust, Christine said, "Oh, shut up, you little weasel, no one's gonna hurt you. Stop blubbering so we can read you your rights."

"We then took Vargas outside and told the other cops that

we had him," she says. "And that was the end of that. We had him cold."

Under a plea bargain agreement, Vargas later pleaded guilty to four of the twenty-two rapes and was sentenced to forty-eight years in prison.

"I really wasn't scared during the entire operation, because it all went so smoothly," Christine says. "Later, when I thought about it, I realized that it had in fact been a real scary business. But it felt real good to get that little pervert off the street."

In 1986, Detective Christine Bridges was honored by the International Association of Police Chiefs and *Parade* magazine when she received Honorable Mention during the Police Officer of the Year Awards.

"I went to Nashville and got a real nice plaque for my wall," she says. "It was very exciting and I enjoyed myself immensely."

Christine also met the redoubtable Special Agent Ed Mireles, who was Police Officer of the Year, and the other fighting FBI agents who had survived the Miami shootout— and even got her picture taken with FBI Chief William Webster.

"At the time I didn't know who he was," she says. "I thought he was just another cop. I said to him, 'Who do you work for, Bill?' and he said, 'The FBI.' I said, 'I'm sure you do a good job,' and he smiled and said, 'Well, I try to.'

"I only learned later that he ran the entire Bureau."

OFFICER GREG ARMSTRONG
Tallahassee, Florida, Police Department

■■■■■■■■■■■■■■■■■■■■■

There are many things you can teach a rookie police officer. You can teach him respect for the laws he enforces and how to deal with the often ungrateful public he is sworn to protect and serve. You can teach him the value of mental preparation so that in the future he can survive a lethal encounter with a ruthless criminal. You can teach a rookie the practice of arms, the care and use of weapons, the when and how of applied deadly force.

All these things can be taught.

But honesty, integrity and compassion you cannot teach. A man or woman is born with these, or they are developed by parents early in childhood.

Similarly, cool, calculating bravery under fire and the instinctive, fine-tuned skills of the gunfighter are not learned. A man or woman is also born with these. They can not be taught on the firing range.

Such skills are rare.

Maybe one cop in a hundred has them in full measure. Experienced police officers will tell you they are rarer still, possessed by perhaps one in a thousand.

Medal-of-Valor-winner Greg Armstrong is such a rarity, a twenty-three-year-old rookie officer just two months out of police college who proved during the course of a raging, sixty-round gunfight that courage and skill-at-arms depend neither on age nor experience . . . These are exceptional gifts bestowed by the jealous gods on a precious few of us.

■   ■   ■

Officer Armstrong of the Tallahassee Police wrote his own heroic chapter in his department's 147-year history of law enforcement on the morning of July 8, 1988, as the citizens of Florida's state capital battened down doors and windows, cranked up air conditioners and prepared for the onslaught of another day of ninety-degree heat and mind-numbing humidity.

On the roadways short-tempered salesmen from out of town, hopelessly snarled in rush-hour traffic, juggled steaming styrofoam coffee cups and cigarettes, cursing the heat, the roads and the city's burgeoning automobile population. Hot and sticky, the drummers glared enviously at pert and pretty secretaries, seemingly as cool as mint, who took advantage of the three and four traffic-light delays to touch up lipstick and hair, using skewed rearview mirrors in a way General Motors and Mr. Toyota never intended.

Greg Armstrong was also battling traffic. He glanced at his watch and saw that it was a few minutes after eight. He had just received a call from Dispatch telling him to respond to a report of a suspicious car parked behind the Lake Bradford Coin Laundry on Lake Bradford Road, next to the Express Lane convenience store.

"It was a routine call, the kind of thing we get every day," Armstrong says. "When I arrived at the location, I saw that Officer Ernest Ponce de Leon was already there. He had arrived a few seconds earlier and was parked near this 1985 olive-green Chevy Impala which was sitting between the Laundromat and the convenience store.

"Ponce smiled and waved a greeting, then we both got out

of our cars and walked up to the Chevy. We later learned that the occupants of the car never saw us arrive, so we came as a complete surprise to them."

Armstrong walked up to the left front door of the car and started to talk to the driver, twenty-six-year-old Henry Joseph Goins. Officer Ponce de Leon made his way to the rear of the vehicle and called in the license tag number, asking for it to be run through the computer, a routine procedure.

"Meantime I was interviewing the driver," Armstrong says. "It was the usual stuff: Where have you been? Where are you going? Do you have any identification?

"The driver said, 'Yeah, I got some identification.' Then he fumbled around for a few minutes. Then he said, 'Well, it's in the trunk.' I said, 'Okay, can you get it for me?'

"The driver got out of the car, went to the trunk and got out one of those small overnight bags. He then walked back to the front of the car, laid the case on the driver's seat and started to rummage through it. Ponce was still standing at the rear of the Impala, waiting for information on the car."

There were four people in the Impala. Henry Goins, described as a white male, Beverly Lee Harris, thirty-nine, a black female, and two other black males, thirty-three-year-old Clarence James Jones and Irvin Griffen, twenty-eight. At that time, Ponce de Leon and Armstrong had no way of knowing that the three men were all escapees from the Maryland House of Corrections in Baltimore, and had stolen the olive-green Impala from the prison motor pool.

"Goins finished looking through his bag and said, 'I can't find my ID,'" Armstrong recalls. "He then turned to Beverly Harris and asked, 'Do you know where it is?' The woman said she thought it was in her makeup case, which was in the trunk.

"Goins went back to the trunk again and got this small overnight case that women often carry, brought it back to the front of the car and he and Beverly Harris started digging through it. Of course, as I later learned, Goins never had any identification. He was stalling, playing for time.

"As he and the woman were rummaging through the case, I don't know what made me look up, but I did. Maybe it was a sixth sense, a feeling that something was going wrong. I looked across the roof of the car and saw Clarence Jones get out of the front passenger door. He was holding a six-inch-barreled Ruger revolver which he leveled at Ponce. He then shot Ponce twice in the chest."

The forty-year-old officer fell to the ground, dying.

"I saw the gun recoil," Armstrong says, "but I didn't hear it. I was only about six feet away, but I didn't hear the bangs. I saw Ponce go down and thought, 'Oh my God, what's happening now?'

"For some reason I didn't attempt to draw my gun. I ran to the corner of the Laundromat to put the building between me and the men in the car. After shooting Ponce, Jones turned and fired at me. He fired four rounds. Three went into the roof of his car and one struck the side of the Laundromat. Meantime Goins threw his suitcases back in the car, then jumped into the front seat. He fumbled with the keys, getting ready to start the Impala.

"Griffen then started shooting from the right rear passenger seat of the car, using a .380 Beretta. He accidentally shot Beverly Harris in the jaw, then put two rounds into the Laundromat wall.

"I believe the men in the car thought they'd got me or that I'd run away. They didn't seem to be in a great hurry to get going, and they didn't come after me. They really weren't looking out for me to come back around the corner of the building."

But Armstrong did come back, suddenly appearing like an avenging angel, his Smith and Wesson Model 586, loaded with six 148-grain, .38 Special+Ps, two-handed up to eye level.

"I came back around the corner, and I saw Jones, the guy who'd shot Ponce, standing next to the Impala," the young cop says. "After he'd shot Ponce, he'd walked over and taken Ponce's gun out of its holster, a 9mm Beretta 92F. He was about to get back into the passenger seat of the car when I shot him. I hit him in the face, and his head disappeared from view.

"Goins had his back turned to me, and he was scrambling around between the front seats of the car. To me, it looked like he was getting a gun. He then turned round and faced me, and I shot him in the neck. I thought I'd killed him. But he survived.

"Jones was now in the front seat of the car, and I fired several more rounds at him through the windshield. I couldn't tell if I'd hit him or not, but I saw his head duck under the dashboard. I thought I'd killed Goins, but he was very much alive. He had managed to start the car, and I knew that if they drove past the corner of the Laundromat, I'd be out in the open. My gun was now empty. I reloaded, putting six more in, then moved my position and stood next to this big old yellow '72 Chrysler that was parked in front of the Laundromat.

"The Impala, trying to get away from there, drove past me. Jones was shooting at me from the front of the car, and Griffen was firing from the backseat. Because of the angle of the Chrysler, they had maybe half-a-second to get me as they drove past. I returned fire and hit Goins in the head. The Impala skidded wildly, then crashed into a vehicle that was parked in front of the Express Lane convenience store.

"My gun was empty again, and I reloaded. Griffen swung open the door of the Impala and ran for the tree line behind the convenience store. Backing up a ways, at this point I didn't know where Officer Ponce De Leon was. I hadn't seen him since the first shots were fired, but I was pretty sure he was down and wounded. Griffen was running and I knew he was armed. I thought maybe he was trying to outflank me, so I fired at him, and hit him smack in the butt."

This was truly excellent combat marksmanship. Officer Armstrong made that shot, at a running target, in the heat of battle, at a distance of thirty-three yards. Up until that time all his practice, and qualifying, with his service revolver had been done at the fifteen-yard line of the police range.

"I saw Griffen stumble and go down after I hit him, then he got up and vanished into the trees," Armstrong says. "After that everything got quiet. I saw that Goins was still in the car, but I didn't know where the other black male and the woman were. I still had not seen or heard from Officer Ponce De Leon.

"I knew then that I had to find Ponce. I walked around the Laundromat, keeping the building between me and the suspects' car. As I walked, I got on my radio and asked for backup and an ambulance because I knew Ponce had to be hurt."

When the backup units arrived, they took Goins, who was still trying to reach for his gun, into custody. Beverly Harris had fled, or was pushed, underneath Officer Ponce de Leon's police car when the shooting started, and that's where the police found her.

Meantime Griffen and Jones had met up with each other. Leaving a trail of blood through the woods behind the convenience store, the two crossed Levy Avenue into Warwick Street, a few hundred yards from the scene of the gunfight, where they tried to enter several houses. The two wounded gunmen then broke into a house on the 2000 block of Warwick where two young boys, aged nine and twelve, were alone. When the kids spotted the blood-splashed men and their guns, they ran to a neighbor's house, where they called the police.

Officers surrounded the house at 2017 Warwick Street and captured the crestfallen suspects without a fight.

Later Goins underwent emergency brain surgery at Tallahassee Memorial Regional Medical Center, and Griffen was also hospitalized there. Jones and Harris were treated for their face wounds and then sent to the Leon County Jail after questioning.

The escapees had been on the loose from the Maryland prison since June 25. They had robbed a convenience store in Richmond, Virginia, on June 28, and the Express Lane convenience store had been chosen as their next target.

Store manager Susie Jones says she wasn't upset by the gunfight, until it was all over. "My clerk told me they could have come in here and taken us hostage, and that's when I lost control," she says.

"I heard the noise outside, but I didn't realize it was gunshots. I thought it was somebody hitting the dumpster."

Jones says that when she walked outside and saw the policeman, she realized she was hearing gunfire. The woman then hid in the store cooler, but got out a few moments later, intending to lock the front door.

"When I got out, I saw one of the suspects crouched down next to my car," she recalls. "He was carrying a gun. When I got clear up almost to the door, and realized he was right in front of me, I got back into the cooler."

Sixty rounds had been fired during the five-second gunfight, and the scene was messy. Nearby cars were shot up, and the inside of the Impala was drenched with blood.

Officer Armstrong stayed with the dying Ponce De Leon till help arrived. "The paramedics told me they detected a faint heartbeat," the young cop says. "But I couldn't really tell what was happening. I was shaking all over and couldn't understand what they were saying to me. I heard the words, but couldn't make any sense out of them. Later I was told that Ponce had died within a few minutes of reaching the hospital."

Henry Joseph Goins later pleaded guilty to second degree murder and received a long prison term. Jones and Griffen stood trial on first degree murder charges. Griffen was given a life sentence and Jones got the death penalty. Jones is still on death row, and his appeals process is expected to last till the end of this century. Beverly Harris, who was used as a state witness in the case, was not charged.

"I survived this gunfight because of luck and because of my training," Armstrong says. "It's very difficult to shoot accurately with a handgun, and that's where my training came in. I had been taught to concentrate on the front sight and squeeze, not jerk, the trigger, and that's what helped save my life.

"Police training is really hard, but it pays off when a cop finds himself in a lethal confrontation. I was taught tactical things, like the best use of cover, and changing cover if the occasion demanded it.

"The training was still fresh in my mind, and that also helped. I hadn't had time to get bored with the job, and nothing was routine. I was on edge all the time. Ponce was the senior officer on our squad, a very experienced cop, so even being with him that day made me on edge. I wanted to do everything right while he was there."

On August 24, 1988, Officer Greg Armstrong was awarded the Medal of Valor, the Tallahassee Police Department's highest award for bravery. A year later, the Committee of 99, a group of private citizens who each year honor law enforcement officers, bestowed its eighth annual Officer of the Year Award on the young rookie.

Then Florida Governor Bob Martinez said: "July 8, 1988, was a very sad day for us. We lost a police officer. Greg Armstrong saw his partner shot down. But in the process, it was a day that made us proud. It showed us that we have dedicated men and woman, like Greg Armstrong.

"Even under intense pressure, Officer Armstrong disabled three armed suspects, called for backup and kept sight of his objectives. His actions have reinforced the confidence the citizens of Tallahassee feel for the officers who have sworn to protect and serve them."

A pewter sculpture of Officer Ponce de Leon was presented to the Tallahassee police by sculptor and jeweler Diane Sams, and the Committee of 99 created the annual Ernest Ponce de Leon Youth Award in his honor.

SERGEANT STEVE CHANEY
Baton Rouge, Louisiana, Police Department

■ ■

Other men say of Sergeant Steve Chaney that he's a regular guy, a dedicated police officer and family man, a career cop with the right stuff who has a great deal to give his department and the community he serves.

All of this is true. But Chaney is much more than that. For a man like him, a man who has lived through his own personal hell and come out of it better and stronger, the passage of time changes how he views the memory of his traumatic experience. With time, effort and great personal courage and fortitude, Chaney refocused his thinking, so that the intensity, frequency and duration of disturbing memories were affected by new events of a more positive nature. But his goal was not to forget. His goal was to file away those memories in the dark recesses of his mind, so that they were no longer an inhibiting factor in his life.

For Steve Chaney, now a sergeant in Louisiana's Baton Rouge Police Department, processing those memories became his own personal victory, and in the final analysis, the true measure of a courageous man.

Chaney's moment of truth began when he could not stop a crazy man from killing a rookie officer right before his eyes. The young cop was haunted by that horror for years.

Chaney knew in his heart that he had done everything right that day, done it by the book, done it as well as any man could be expected to do it. But the memory grabbed hold of him and wouldn't let go, so that he slowly began to doubt his own worth as a cop. Then came the day he faced another deadly challenge—and in a lethal, three-second blaze of gunfire rediscovered his value as a police officer and forever laid to rest the ghosts that haunted his past.

■　　■　　■

"If I go back to the day it all began, March 1, 1977, I see Officer Linda Lawrence and me sitting in our car just a few minutes after roll call," Chaney recalls.

"Our first call of the day came in from Dispatch, telling us to attend an attempted burglary at the Broadmore Plantation Apartments, and to meet the complainant at the tennis courts. It was a routine call, one that I'd attended hundreds of times, and there was nothing about it to prepare me for what was to come."

As Chaney drove, Linda Lawrence, blond, lively and extremely pretty, revealed a rookie's lack of enthusiasm for what seemed to be another unexciting start to the day. "Attempted burglary," she sighed. "We'll find a few scratches on the door made by a nervous teenager who couldn't break into a cookie jar."

Chaney smiled. "That's police work. Call it 99.9 percent routine. It's the other .1 percent of the time you have to look out for."

"What is it they used to say in the Army?" Linda asked. "It's 99 percent boredom and 1 percent terror?"

Chaney smiled again, turned to his partner and shook his head. "Yeah, police work is something like that."

"The parking lot was some distance from the woman's apartment, and when Linda and I got there, we did see some small scratches near the lock on the front door, but it didn't appear to have been pried open or anything," Chaney recalls. "In fact it was still locked."

Officer Lawrence went in by the back door and met Chaney on the first floor. Chaney silently jabbed his index finger several times toward the landing at the top of the staircase. "Let's go up and take a look," he whispered.

The two cops made their way up the carpeted staircase to the second floor. After checking the rooms, they approached a bedroom at the end of the hallway. The door was closed.

Chaney pushed the door open and came face-to-face with stocky, big-bellied John James Mullery.

"What are you doing in here?" Chaney demanded. Then, as the man crowded close to him, he ordered, "Hey, back up! Back up!"

Mullery, six feet tall, weighing 210 pounds and obviously in a highly agitated state, screamed, "Why don't you kill me and get it over with? Why don't you just kill me?"

Chaney, a medium-sized man who wears glasses, said that he wasn't there to kill anybody and that he "just wanted to know what was goin' on."

"Get it over with," Mullery said again. "Get your gun out and kill me. I don't care anymore. Get it over with."

"Calm down, relax," Chaney said. "I'm just here to talk to you. I just want to know what you're doing in this house. All I want to do is talk. Just talk."

As Chaney tried to calm down Mullery—who may have been high on PCP or some other drug—the man suddenly lunged for the stainless steel, four-inch-barreled Smith and Wesson in the holster on Chaney's right hip.

"I tried to stiff-arm him away," the cop recalls, "but he kept coming back for my gun. He finally reached it by tearing the holster open, and came up with the gun in his right hand. I slid my hands down and grabbed the cylinder of the weapon so he couldn't pull the trigger. I then tried to wrestle the gun away from him, but couldn't do it. I remember looking back toward Linda, who had drawn her own weapon, and saying, 'I can't get my gun from him. I think you're going to have to shoot him.'"

Wide-eyed, her face totally drained of color, Officer Lawrence fired, the high-velocity .38 Special+P round plowing into Mullery's chest.

"When Linda fired, I felt the shock waves from her weapon hit me on the back of the head," Chaney says, "I'd never seen a man shot up close like that before, and I wasn't prepared for it. I didn't expect the blood and meat that splattered all over, splashing my uniform and hands.

"Now that Mullery had been wounded, I started to fight harder—but I still couldn't get my gun back. The guy was enormously strong, and his blood had gotten all over my hands and all over the gun, and I couldn't keep a grip on the cylinder. Mullery squeezed the trigger and got off a couple of shots which slammed into a wall.

"I was fighting so close with Mullery that Linda probably felt she couldn't get off another shot. She jumped onto the bed with her weapon held out in front of her at eye level. Just then I managed to push Mullery away. I two-handed my revolver and fired two shots into his chest as he went back. When my bullets hit, he flew backward toward Linda, and the back of his right hand hit the back of her right hand."

Chaney couldn't really follow what happened next; it came in a sudden, fast blur of movement. After Mullery's hand hit hers, Linda's gun moved in a semicircle and the butt came into Mullery's hand. The man fired. Linda went down on the bed, shot in the chest, dying within a few seconds.

"I saw the round hit Linda in the chest and knew with awful certainty that she was dead," Chaney says. "After Mullery fired, he and I struggled for both guns. I managed to get control of the two weapons and dropped to my hands and knees, firing both guns into the floor. I was having trouble keeping the guns away from Mullery, so my intention was to empty both of them, and I counted the shots as I fired. I came down to having just one round left in my gun, and Linda's was empty. As Mullery struggled with me on the floor, I threw Linda's gun away, trying to get it out of the apartment window. But as I threw it, Mullery hit me and the gun bounced off the wall.

"As we struggled for possession of my gun, Mullery bit down hard on my finger. I thought, Yeah, keep busy, bite on that for a spell while I find a bone and end this. I reached down with my gun and jammed the muzzle against a bone in Mullery's right rib cage—and fired.

"The .38 Special+P bullet went through Mullery's chest, clean through from side to side, and he said, 'Oh, you got me a good one that time.'

"Then he picked me up and threw me."

Chaney was lifted right off his feet and slammed against a wall, on top of the bedroom dresser. As Mullery got to his feet and came toward him, the desperate cop pointed his Smith at the man and pulled the trigger again and again, hearing only a *click, click, click* as the hammer fell on empty cartridge cases.

Mullery kept coming on, his thick arms spread, a crazed grin on his face.

"I knew I had to get my weapon reloaded, so I jammed myself in a corner and punched out the empty shell cases from the cylinder," Chaney recalls.

"As I fumbled with the reloader, Mullery came up behind me, beating me on the back and head with a tire iron. Then he plunged a kitchen knife into my back. The point of the blade hit one of the ribs on my upper back, and the carbon steel blade bent, saving my life.

"But now I had my weapon reloaded, and I fired once from under my armpit. I saw the round hit Mullery in the solar plexus area, and he staggered backwards. I turned and grabbed him by the hair on the front part of his head and pulled him down to his knees. I then laid the muzzle of the gun on top of his head and fired a round into his brain.

"I remember looking down at his head and seeing the big hole in his skull. I pushed him back and he fell to the floor. I stepped back and leaned gratefully against the dresser, gasping, trying to get my breath back. Then I looked up . . . and Mullery was getting to his feet again.

"To me, it was beyond belief that the man was getting up again, but he really was. I raised my weapon and pointed it at his chest. He was still coming toward me. I fired four rounds into his chest from a range of about six feet and he fell to the floor.

"This time he didn't get up."

After taking a total of ten close-range hits from the 125-grain jacketed hollowpoints in .38 Special+P, including one in the head, across a time span of ten minutes, Mullery finally was down for good. He died seconds later.

Mullery, a thirty-two-year-old housepainter and ex-convict, had not been burglarizing the apartment. He had been waiting for his former girlfriend, planning to beat her to death.

"This was a man who regularly abused women," Chaney says. "He had broken into the apartment some time earlier, waiting there to kill his girlfriend.

"He had built up a tremendous hatred for this woman, and when he was confronted by a female authority figure in Officer Linda Lawrence, well, that's what made him finally crack."

Pretty, blond Linda Lawrence was the first female police officer killed in the line of duty in the state of Louisiana. Thirty years old, she had been a cop for less than two months, and Steve Chaney had been her partner and training officer for less than two weeks.

"Once I realized it was all over, that Linda was dead, I

guess I broke down," Chaney recalls. "I stood there gasping for breath, my whole body trembling, till help arrived. I was hurting all over."

The twenty-six-year-old cop was awarded the Medal of Valor following his terrible battle with John James Mullery, but in the weeks and months to come Chaney tried to answer the questions that came to haunt him. Could he have done the thing better, handled the situation differently? And, above all, when it was all over, why was Linda Lawrence dead and he still alive?

Alone, and without professional help, Chaney tried to come to grips with what had happened, especially the fact that a cop's behavior in a crisis situation can never be predicted with certainty, and that some questions simply don't have answers.

"I eventually got divorced from my first wife," Chaney says. "Since then I've learned that a lot of cops see their marriages break up after a shooting. But I couldn't relate any one incident from the shooting to the breakup of my marriage. It seems that everything just went sour from that point on.

"Probably one of the hardest things I had to deal with later was fear, wondering how many more supernatural people like Mullery were out there, and if I'd ever have to deal with another one."

As he tried to cope with the loss of Linda Lawrence, Chaney received support from an unexpected source, his fellow officers. He found men who were willing to listen, men to whom he could confide his deepest emotions and fears, men who had also been to hell and back.

"Many of my friends were Vietnam veterans, and some of them had lost friends every day," Chaney recalls. "They understood what I was going through, and their reassurance and support helped me through this time."

One of these men was Baton Rouge Police Lieutenant

Mickey Mann. He says: "I spent a year-and-a-half in Vietnam, in heavy combat, and when I got home, I wanted to share my experiences. I wanted to tell what had happened there, maybe it was to help me heal myself, to relieve my guilt over Vietnam.

"For a long time I really couldn't find anyone that I was willing to share with, that I felt I could trust."

Then, in the course of a casual conversation, Officer Chaney and Lieutenant Mann found that they shared the same feelings and many of the same doubts and hurts. Other Vietnam vets also told Chaney that they had lost friends in combat, and had later started the mentally shattering game of second-guessing. Chaney learned that this emotional seesaw was very common among the survivors of Vietnam.

"When we were finished talking, it seemed that a great weight had been taken off Steve's shoulders," Mann says. "It seemed to me he was stepping livelier, that the spring was back in his step and that even the expression on his face had changed for the better.

"I guess he learned that many of us had lost friends in combat. That he wasn't alone. That he could find a willing and understanding ear anytime he wanted to talk about it."

Chaney says that he had by then reached a point where he didn't feel the pain anymore. "I now wanted to win," he says. "I wanted to come out of this terrible experience whole and well."

Steve Chaney's recovery was to be tested five short years later, when he had to face another crisis which required both confidence and courage—and seemed in some ways an eerie replay of what had gone before.

Again the complainant was a woman, who said she was receiving threatening phone calls from a man at a downtown bar. The suspect, Marion Neems, was the same age and had the same occupation as John Mullery. He was, however, much bigger, standing six-feet-eight-inches tall, weighing well over three hundred pounds. It was also known that he regularly carried a gun.

What Steve Chaney didn't know was that Neems had made a solemn vow. "At one time in my life," he'd told friends, "I am going to kill a cop."

But this lethal confrontation was destined to turn out very differently from Chaney's first one. The young cop would control the action from start to finish and quickly and efficiently, and with a great deal of courage, neutralize an extremely deadly threat.

Chaney walked into the bar and asked Neems to step outside into the parking lot. Outdoors, blinking in the sudden sunlight, Neems asked, "Are you going to arrest me?"

Chaney replied, "No, I just want to check out some of the telephone calls you've been making."

"Are you going to arrest me?" Neems asked again.

"Not if I don't have to," Chaney replied. "The lady made a complaint, and I have to submit a report. I just want to talk to you, so just calm down and relax."

Neems's right hand moved slowly toward his back pocket. Chaney warned: "Get your hand out of your pocket! Just stand right there and let me talk to you."

"Are you gonna arrest me?" Neems asked a third time.

Again Chaney replied, "Not if I don't have to. All we have to do right now is talk about the phone calls you've been making."

"I got a gun," Neems said.

Chaney quickly drew his own weapon and said, "Turn around and place your hands on the wall."

Again Neems's hand went to his hip pocket. "Get your hand out of your pocket or I'll have to kill you," Chaney warned. The cop backed up a few steps. "Don't take that gun out of your pocket," he said again.

Neems moved. His right fist came up fast from his pocket. In it he was holding a snub-nosed .38 special.

Chaney quickly two-handed his Smith up to eye level and fired, hitting Neems twice in the chest. A third 140-grain .38 Special+P JHP hit Neems's hand, knocking his gun to the ground. The man fell heavily to the gravel of the parking lot. Bleeding horribly from his devastating wounds, Neems lay there for a few seconds . . . then started to get up, reaching out, thick fingers splayed, for the gun beside him.

In that terrible moment it seemed to Steve Chaney that history was repeating itself, that his nightmare of a few years ago was returning.

"I remember saying to myself, 'Oh no, not me again,'" he recalls. "But it *was* happening again. But, because of my first experience, I was able to make the decision to end this quickly. I fired again, hitting Neems in the throat, cutting his air passage in half and shattering his spinal column. He was instantly paralyzed, and he died in the hospital emergency room an hour later.

"I believe that Marion Neems intentionally committed suicide by police officer, using a cop to pull the trigger to end his life. He could easily have stepped away from this, but the man seemed to have a death wish and just wouldn't quit.

"Afterwards, when I got a chance to think about it, I was glad that I was alive, glad that I'd handled the situation, glad I wasn't injured and glad that I hadn't lost anyone this time.

"It seems to me that many of life's positive lessons are not learned in positive ways."

Chaney's attractive, hazel-eyed wife, Debra, says: "Naturally I was really worried about how this second incident would affect Steve. I knew that after the first incident his first marriage had ended, but that experience, and the lessons he learned from it, had improved his coping skills.

He had come to realize that life throws people some curves, that there is nothing predictable about life.

"Life is difficult, and Steve knows that. But now he has found the wonderful ability to share his feelings and emotions with others in a very special way.

"What seems like the worst tragedies in our life may actually be opportunities for growth and a time for new beginnings and a time to appreciate your loved ones in a very different way.

"Steve and I have found that it sometimes takes the depths of despair to know the heights of happiness. Sometimes you need to feel very bad in order to feel very good.

"I want Steve to know that I'm still with him, still close to him. Touching is important, letting him know that I'm still one with him. He needs to know that, no matter what, we can face it together.

"Today, we go from one step, to the next step, to the next . . . and eventually the healing takes place."

Steve Chaney is now assigned to the Baton Rouge Police Department's Second District, where he works day shift.

"It's busy there, and I enjoy it," he says. "I find police work rewarding, and I love the interaction with people.

"I now see a future for me in law enforcement, and I sincerely believe that I can make a difference."

OFFICER GERO
Gainesville, Florida, Police Department

■ ■ ■ ■ ■ ■ ■ ■ ■ ■ ■ ■

Near this spot are deposited the remains of one who possessed
Beauty without Vanity,
Strength without Insolence,
Courage without Ferocity
And all the Virtues of man without his Vices.
This praise, which would be unmeaning Flattery if inscribed over human ashes,
Is but a just tribute to the memory . . . of a Dog.

The great English poet Lord George Byron neatly summed up the character of the ideal dog when he wrote this touching epitaph for a departed friend and faithful companion some 160 years ago.

Today, Byron's heartfelt little tribute accurately describes the ideal police dog . . . and in particular a valiant, faithful German shepherd named Gero, a dog who gave his own life to save that of his fellow officers.

In common with other canine units across the nation, Florida's Gainesville Police Department gives its dogs the rank of police officers. They have their own badges and their own pension and retirement plans, so that when the bright doggy eyes grow dim and the wet noses smell less and less, they will be well cared for in their old age.

Gero, who was just six years old when he was killed, was destined never to grow old. But his sacrifice will always be remembered by his fellow officers, and his name is still mentioned whenever cops speak of devotion to duty and bravery under fire.

During a dazzling four-year career on the Gainesville PD, Gero, trained by his handler Officer Mike Pruitt, was credited with seventeen solo arrests and forty-eight assists. His record included the apprehension of a rapist, fifty-seven burglars, three auto thieves and two men who had assaulted police officers.

Gero—his name is Apache and means "he who walks in his shadow"—also found two missing children, a two-year-old who had wandered away from a nursery, and a seven-year-old who had gotten lost.

"He went right to both of those kids, just like he knew where they were at," says Pruitt. "He had an instinctive talent for that kind of police work."

Gero was compelled to use force only once in his career, when he pinned down an armed burglar at a discount store on South Main Street. The dog then went on to recover $300,000 worth of stolen jewelry.

Pruitt always made sure that Gero got a treat after he'd made an arrest. "We'd stop at a 7-Eleven where the owner kept a supply of frozen Snickers bars," he says. "I'd break one in half and share it with Gero, just to let him know that he'd done good. It was a little enough reward, but it was always the highlight of Gero's day. I know it's not advisable to give a dog chocolate, but Gero seemed to thrive on it."

The big, black-and-tan shepherd loved children, and a peewee fan club would gather at the 7-Eleven every time he showed up. Gero took their patting and petting without complaint, patiently allowing little hands to rub his head and pull his ears as the kids showed their rough and ready appreciation for a beautiful and friendly animal.

Gero made his last arrest a few days before he died. He helped apprehend a burglary suspect at Gainesville's First Baptist Church. The man was hiding on the roof of the building, but as soon as he saw the huge dog purposely padding toward him, he quickly threw up his hands and surrendered.

"Most of the time, when the police dog arrives on the scene, the suspects just give up," Pruitt says.

But on the last day of Gero's life, that pattern was to be tragically broken.

On Friday, January 24, 1986, a few minutes after midnight, members of the Gainesville PD Special Operations Unit— plainclothes officers who work special details—spotted twenty-nine-year-old Darrell Earl Parker riding a bicycle in the area just north of the downtown plaza on Northeast First Street. When the SOU officers saw Parker, who had a history of felony convictions dating back to 1973, enter the law office of attorney David Cox at 618 Northeast First Street, they radioed for assistance from uniformed patrol officers.

A perimeter of eight officers, including Pruitt with Gero, was set up around the building while Parker ransacked the rooms inside.

An officer in front of the building then cupped his hands to his mouth and yelled to Parker: "The building is surrounded by police officers. Come out slowly with your hands in the air."

Parker, whose record included burglary, aggravated assault and possession of a firearm during the commission of a felony, immediately burst through the back door of the law office, which opened onto a small elevated porch.

The police officers yelled for the man to halt. But in

reply, Parker snapped off a quick shot at Officer Steve Baker from his .32-caliber handgun.

"The canine Gero was right there," Deputy Chief Larry Gabbard said later. "He responded as he'd been trained to respond and leaped onto the suspect. The dog took Parker's attention away from firing at the other officers. Had the dog not been willing to sacrifice his life, one or more of the police officers present could have died."

Parker fired twice at the leaping dog, both bullets striking Gero in the body. The big shepherd grabbed hold of Parker's wrist, but the gunman fired again, the round crashing between Gero's shoulders.

"Oh God, no!" Pruitt screamed, running toward Parker. But it was too late. The impact of Parker's last round knocked Gero into Pruitt, and he fell with the dog in his lap. Parker now steadied himself and squeezed off another two-handed round at Pruitt. The bullet slammed into Gero. The dog yelped and lay still.

"Gero took the bullet that was meant for me," Pruitt said later. "I would have taken that round in my chest or groin."

Officers Pruitt and Baker returned fire. Parker was hit four times, twice in the heart, once in the shoulder and once in the hand. He fell heavily to the porch, dying within seconds.

Gero too was dying. He later passed away in his handler's arms, dying as he'd lived, bravely and without complaint.

The dog's death was announced to other police departments that morning, "on the police teletype, as any officer's death would be announced," said Deputy Chief Gabbard.

Sergeant Butch Taylor, who was then in charge of the Gainesville Police K-9 unit, waited a few days before making arrangements for Gero's funeral.

"We were sad to lose him," Taylor says. "And we were proud that he made the sacrifice he did to save two officers' lives. But we couldn't overlook the fact that a human being had died too. Out of respect for the dead man's family, we didn't want to hold Gero's funeral on the same day."

The Gainesville PD gave Gero a hero's funeral on January 29, 1986, five days after he died. More than two hundred people attended the ceremony, including fifty police officers from all over Florida and six police dogs.

Lieutenant Norbert Thomas of the canine unit stood in the weak winter sunshine at the Gainesville Police Academy and solemnly read from "A Tribute to a Dog":

"He guards the sleep of his master as if he were a prince. And when death takes the master in its embrace . . . there by his graveside will the noble dog be found."

Police Chief Wayland Clifton spoke of "valor above and beyond the call of duty," and "giving one's life for a friend." Then he added: "Gero did exactly as he was trained to do, and he paid the ultimate price."

Before the white, flag-draped casket was lowered into the ground, Officer Mike Pruitt, a black band across his badge, looked away from the small coffin to the blue sky above the pine trees. He was a man struggling with his emotions, but he was first and foremost a policeman.

"Gero was my partner," he said simply. "I depended on him and he depended on me."

As the casket was lowered into the earth, the fifty police officers present snapped to attention and saluted, their last tribute to an honored hero.

As the dog was laid to rest, an unwrapped Snickers bar lay next to his head. It had been placed there a few minutes earlier by Officer Pruitt.

It was Pruitt's way of telling Gero that he'd done good.